The Yonderley Boy

BRIAN MORSE

The Yonderley Boy

Glover & Blair Limited

For Daniel, Lisa, and Wendy, my wife

First published in Great Britain by
Glover & Blair Limited,
Kings Place, 329 Chiswick High Road, London W4

Set in Plantin by Book Economy Tapeset Ltd.
Printed and bound in Great Britain by
Tonbridge Printers Limited
Peach Hall Works
Tonbridge, Kent

ISBN 0 906681 01 4

I

From his bedroom window Johnny watched the lane that laboured up the hill below the back of his house and up which his friend Daniel would come. Then he lifted his eyes to let them rove over the hill that faced him. Denver Hill, or Denver as it was known locally, filled the view. High and steep and without houses, the hill's top was covered by a dense wood. Below the trees it was parcelled out into fields which were farmed by Mr Butler, Daniel's father. The farm buildings, however, were hidden from view by a row of elms on the other side of the lane from Johnny's, as was the bottom of the valley and an old disused canal that ran along it and into a tunnel under the hill.

It was early for Daniel to arrive, but that Saturday morning Johnny expected him earlier than usual. It had been Daniel's birthday during the week, and last night he had gone into town with his father to collect the bike that was to be his big present. Johnny did not have to wait long. As the clock on Summerfield Church tower began to strike the quarter hour at the front of the house, a cyclist appeared on the lane, standing on his pedals to get the most out of his effort as he toiled up the last hundred yards to Johnny's garden.

Johnny lingered at the window for a moment. He wanted to see how well the bike went. Johnny thought that Daniel came over the rise and onto the flatter bit by the garden gate with just that little bit more ease than he would have managed on his own bike. Then Daniel put on a little spurt of speed and began impatiently ringing his bell in summons. Johnny left the window and rushed downstairs.

'Daniel's come,' he called from the hall. 'I'm going out.'

'Don't slam the back door like you've just slammed your bedroom one,' his Dad complained from behind the morning newspaper. 'I'm sick of hearing Mum say it.'

'Okay,' Johnny replied. 'I was in a hurry.'

He ran down the garden path and was at the gate scarcely before Daniel had dismounted.

The two didn't bother saying hello.

'How does it go?' Johnny said. 'I watched you coming up the rise.'

'Smashing. A dream. I did the whole trip in five minutes flat.'

Johnny considered. 'I've done it faster.'

'Perhaps,' Daniel replied. 'But I hardly wanted to go flat-out the first time I rode it.'

They both looked at the gleaming new machine, Daniel with pride, Johnny with a tinge of envy.

'Well,' he said, 'I'll tell Mum we're off. I suppose you do want to go for a spin?'

'Do you think I don't?' Daniel said. 'You'll see which is faster then!'

'Rubbish! Mine'll beat yours hollow any day!'

Actually there wasn't much in it between the two bikes. Because of its better gears Daniel's had the edge over Johnny's uphill, but Johnny's was just as fast on the flat. All this was secret relief to Johnny who'd been worried, without saying anything to his friend, that Daniel's bike would be superior. He was proud of his own, though by now it was rather scratched and dented, not at all the gleaming new one it had once been, and he didn't want to feel ashamed of it for any reason.

They spent the morning around Summerfield, racing from one spot to another and dashing down the lane to the farm and back, then finished up at Johnny's to watch the end of the morning programmes on television. Daniel went home for dinner. But after dinner they both felt more ambitious. Surely with two good bikes now they could try something out of the ordinary? Why not a trip further afield than usual?

It had turned from a hot morning into a very hot afternoon. At dinner Dad had said it promised to be the hottest day of the year so far. The sun beat down and the air really smelt of summer. Until now the weather had been most unpredictable – only ten days before it had thundered and lightninged over Denver and the ground had been sodden for ages.

The two were in the road at the front of Johnny's house, on Summerfield's main street. Johnny was sitting on the gate gazing at the church tower; Daniel was staring at the house adjoining Johnny's. It had a 'For Sale' notice in the garden with the name of an estate agent in town; a smaller notice tacked to it read 'Rent Considered'.

'Your other house has been up for sale for ages,' Daniel said.

'Nearly a year.'

'Doesn't anyone want it?'

'People come to look sometimes,' Johnny replied, 'but Mum says Dad's asking too much.'

'And is he?'

'He might be. The trouble is Mum and Dad don't fancy new neighbours. They put people off.' He turned to stare too. 'Some people have come I've really liked.'

The two stone-built houses were identical, from the bedrooms upstairs to the front and back rooms and the kitchen. Only the colour of the paintwork was different. Great-Uncle Jim had left the house to Mum and Dad in his will, which was no surprise since Mum had been nursing him for years. He would have been ninety this year and Johnny only remembered him as a bed-ridden old man. His furniture was still inside, the best of it hidden under dust-covers. Johnny used to go and peer through the windows sometimes and try to make out individual objects in the gloom, but he never stayed long. To his mind the house was a bit eery now it was unlived in, 'spooky' he used to say though Dad told him not to be so silly. Dad was a firm disbeliever in spirits or ghosts or anything of the kind.

A car came up the back lane at that moment, its engine

protesting at the climb, and stopped where the lane joined the road. It was visible over Great-Uncle Jim's garden wall. It stayed there till the driver chose left and then went on, away from the village.

'We ought to do something special today,' Daniel said, 'to celebrate my new bike. It's no use just sitting here hoping something will come along.'

'There are dozens of places.' Johnny yawned lazily, putting his face up to catch the sun.

'Okay, but which one?'

'You choose. It's your birthday.'

'Somewhere out of the ordinary. Let's follow that car into town.'

'All that traffic,' Johnny said, 'and it takes Dad half an hour to get there driving. How long would it take us by bike? Anyway, we go that way to school every day of the week. What about somewhere in the country? That would be the nicest. Somewhere we don't usually go. Mind you, not too far. I'm supposed to be in earlyish tonight – Mum and Dad are going out.'

'I know! The canal!' Daniel said.

'The canal on the way to the farm? We can go down there any time, and we wouldn't need our bikes.'

'Not this end, stupid,' Daniel shouted. He jumped off his perch into the road.

'What end then?'

'The other, of course, where the tunnel comes out. And it won't be too far.'

'At Yonderley you mean?' Yonderley was the hamlet the back lane led to past the Butler's farm. It was over the other side of Denver. 'I've never been to the other end of the canal tunnel.'

'There you are,' Daniel said triumphantly. 'I've solved it. Dad took me and Mum there once, ages ago. It'll be somewhere really different.'

'Where is it?' Johnny asked, puzzled. 'Exactly.' He'd never thought of the canal tunnel coming out anywhere, only accepted it was there. 'I know it's near Yonderley, but how would we get there?'

'Dad took us there by road,' Daniel explained. 'But I'm sure we could find it by cutting across country. We could use the bikes most of the way. The track that goes up Denver to the woods through our farm would probably bring us out very close to it.'

'Right – you're on,' Johnny said, jumping down into the road too. 'I don't know why we've never been there, but it's about time we did. Race you?'

2

They turned down the lane at the corner by Great Uncle Jim's, and gathered speed as they passed Johnny's back gate. They kept well into the left for a car coming up would have filled the narrow lane and met them head-on. A hundred yards from the bottom the lane straightened out and they hit the hump-backed canal bridge at full speed. The bikes were thrown into the air on the crown of the bridge so that for a moment they had the sensation of flying. They were going so fast that they only had to touch their pedals just before they reached the turning to the Butlers'. They turned right onto the farm's gravelled drive and in a moment they were dismounting at the yard-gate. Once in the farm-yard they headed for the kitchen. After a moment's haggling Daniel's mother handed over a bottle of lemonade.

'Where are you off to?' she called after them from the kitchen door as they bolted out of the door again.

'Over the top of Denver,' Daniel called back.

'Not *too* far over,' she shouted.

'Don't worry,' Daniel called over his shoulder. 'Mum still seems to think there are people waiting to waylay you up there,' he said to Johnny.

'Were there?'

'Once upon a time. This track over the hill used to be important. There was a famous highwayman who robbed people in the woods.'

The track zig-zagged its way up through the fields above the farm. Soon the house and the out-buildings surrounding it looked small below them. The taller and longer-legged Daniel led the way. His mop of red hair bobbed up and down through the ruts ahead of Johnny. Johnny in contrast was a shorter, dark-haired lad.

Twenty-five minutes later they neared the top of Denver. It had been hard work. They had opened and closed half a dozen gates on the way up, but now only one enormous field remained before they reached the final gate which marked the boundary of Mr Butler's land.

Johnny remounted his bike, then leant over the gate they'd just come through. From here he could see all the way down to the farm buildings and over the fields, several of which were dotted with sheep. In another field he spotted Mr Butler's herd of prize-winning cattle. It was quiet, with only the occasional bleat of sheep or call of a bird.

Well below their level lay Summerfield, its houses and roads spread out on the top of its own hill like the model of a village instead of the village itself. Johnny fancied he could see Dad on their back doorstep but the dot he saw could have been Mum or even a neighbour knocking at the door. Beyond the low hill on which Summerfield stood there were other hilltops and villages and the town, too, but the details were lost in the shimmering air. One thing you could not see from here was the canal tunnel entrance. It and the canal were hidden by the overhang of the hill.

Daniel let Johnny stand a couple of minutes, then he cycled on and called Johnny to follow him. 'It's odd to think there's a tunnel right under us,' he shouted. 'Mind you, there's a lot of dirt and rock between us and it. No danger of it not bearing our weight.'

'I wasn't worried!' Johnny grinned.

The ground evened out at last. They were approching Denver's flat top and suddenly the woods they'd not seen since leaving Johnny's were in sight. Johnny looked back over his shoulder. That way only the clear blue sky and the stone wall that bounded the last field were visible. They had still not quite reached the top of the hill but the farm and the village had vanished completely.

'It's easier riding now,' he called to Daniel. He began to pedal furiously. 'Race you!' he shouted as he passed his friend. Then they reached the last gate. When they'd closed it behind them they were in totally unfamiliar territory.

The woods looked really neglected and unvisited. Other hikers must have been this way earlier in the year — Johnny himself had seen a man and a woman with rucksacks on their backs using the right of way through the farmyard a couple of weekends before — but not many of them, and it felt as if they were the first visitors for ages.

A bird flew chattering across the track in front of them. Johnny, who was in the lead, almost fell off his bike with surprise.

The track was full of hidden bumps and pot-holes. It certainly wasn't made for racing on. At one point a tree brought down by some autumn gale still lay intact across their path. They dismounted and pulled the bikes over. Then the track mounted over a little ridge and started steeply downwards. Ahead was just a sea of trees. Leaves brushed their faces and wiry branches whipped them. It would have been perfect ambush territory for Daniel's highwaymen!

Suddenly the ground fell away on their right. Daniel, in the lead now, jumped off his bike. There was a drop of many feet to the bottom of a little tree-filled valley which cut into the main hillside.

Johnny got off his bike too. 'Is this where the canal comes out?' he asked.

'I'd think so,' Daniel said, 'though I can't see it down there with all those trees.'

They laid their bikes on their sides and crouched at the edge of the drop. The valley was perhaps three hundred yards across with cliffs all the way round.

'I feel quite dizzy,' Johnny said. 'I hope you're not thinking of climbing down.'

'It hadn't entered my mind!' Daniel said. 'If you fell on the way down, I'd hate to think what would happen to you. Just look at those rocks down there. Anyway, there's sure to be an entrance to the valley lower down.'

'Come on, let's find it then,' Johnny said. 'It looks great down there — a kind of hidden valley.'

They wheeled their bikes a hundred yards or so until the track went back among trees both sides, then remounted. The track went over another ridge, then down more gently. Standing on their pedals, the two boys coasted down. Soon the track ran into a lane.

'Right!' Daniel called. 'It must be!'

They gathered speed on the smoother tarmac, though to judge by the grass which grew down its middle the lane wasn't used much more than the track. They went down and round the curve and at the bottom was a little hump-backed bridge just like the one below Johnny's. The canal did indeed come out through the little valley.

A towpath led along the left-hand side of the canal.

'It's even more overgrown than on our side of Denver,' Daniel said. 'I don't think we'll be able to use our bikes along there at all.'

Johnny looked over the parapet of the bridge. The bed of the canal was full of brambles and long coarse grass. A dank rotten smell came off it, for it was wet beneath the undergrowth even though the sun was baking hot at the moment. As for the towpath Daniel was certainly right about that. They were going to have to walk.

'It's difficult to imagine boats used to sail along here once,' Johnny said. 'Just as it's difficult to imagine coaches and carts once used that track over the hill.'

'It must have always been an out of the way place over here,' Daniel agreed. 'If you go on down the lane it's probably miles before you reach a house.'

They hid their bikes from view just to be on the safe side, though they'd seen no one since leaving the farm. Then they began walking along the towpath. In a minute the lane was hidden from sight as the canal curved round to keep midway between the sides of the little valley. Up on the right, hidden among the trees at the top of the rising cliffs, would be the track they had followed over the hill.

'It can't be very far to the tunnel mouth,' Johnny said. 'Is there anything else to see when we get there?'

'I can't really remember.' Daniel scratched his head. 'It's ages since I came here. There was a little old cottage that Dad wouldn't let me go in.' Suddenly he began to run. 'Race you!' he called.

The towpath became more and more overgrown. Plant life had filled in every available square inch of space. They had to leap over bramble branches to keep going. It got darker, too. Johnny glanced up as he ran. The trees seemed to lean together and meet overhead as if they were making a roof — especially when he ran fast. He put on an extra burst of speed to catch up and ran straight into Daniel who had stopped dead.

'What did you do that for?'

'I don't know,' Daniel replied. 'It's odd — '

'What is?'

'I don't know. Just something.'

He shrugged and continued on his way, Johnny close at his heels. The towpath mounted and then levelled out as they passed a single lock on its own, the wood rotten and splintering after years of neglect. Johnny glanced uneasily around. Daniel had put into words a sense of unease he'd felt himself, the reason why he'd rushed to catch his friend up. He glanced up again at the dense cover of branches through which the sky only showed occasionally. There was a wisp of cloud that seemed more misty than the sharply etched white clouds outside the wood, but Johnny stumbled and paid no more attention to it because the way along the path was becoming more slippery where the mud had not dried. Suddenly it felt cold too. Johnny found himself shivering.

'Is the tunnel mouth far now?' he whispered. For no reason his nerves were all on edge.

'I don't remember,' Daniel said. 'I shouldn't think so. It's not very nice in here, is it? It's quite different our side of Denver. It doesn't get so much sun, I suppose, with those cliffs all around.'

The lock was behind them and out of sight round another bend when they came to a small clearing where the trees didn't crowd so closely up to the path. There was room for low bushes to grow. Johnny wouldn't have given them a second glance had not Daniel suddenly pulled up short again.

'What is it?' Johnny said.

'Look — these brambles,' Daniel said in an amazed tone of voice, pulling a thick, richly-laden stem towards him.

'What's strange?' Johnny queried. 'It seems all right to me. Those blackberries look luscious.' He bent down to pick one. 'By far the best thing we've seen since leaving the road if you want my opinion. Down here may have looked exciting from above, but there's something about down here I don't like at all.'

'But the blackberries are ripe!' Daniel said.

'So what?'

'Think!' Daniel said in exasperation. 'What month is it?'

'July.'

'Are blackberries usually ripe this time of year? It's not possible for them to be ripe now, especially somewhere as shady as this.'

Johnny put a fruit in his mouth, puzzled over it a moment, then spat it out.

'It was completely tasteless.' He shuddered.

'I could have told you it would taste like that,' Daniel said in a 'told-you-so' tone. 'I know not much sun gets down here, but all the same you wouldn't expect it to be so cool, would you? And have you noticed how wet the ground is?'

They gazed around, suddenly searching for what was wrong because there definitely was something wrong about the little valley.

A leaf, half dowdy green, half brown, drifted down and settled in the mud at their feet, then a whole shower of leaves. There were bare branches above them.

Suddenly they both realised what was wrong.

July it might be outside this dark wood, but inside they had been plunged into a cool, damp autumn day. But it was two months off autumn yet!

3

'It's all totally wrong!' Daniel was gazing round in amazement. 'Not just the blackberries, but everything — the trees, the bushes, the air, the way the ground is. What can have caused it?'

'It's cold, too,' Johnny added. 'That's what I noticed first. The temperature's like it is in October, when my birthday is.'

'Like autumn. Your're right. But what's caused the cold?' Daniel went on. 'Something's made it colder here than anywhere else. It hasn't just happened.'

'It seems very sheltered here,' Johnny said. 'Even if this valley gets less sun, it won't get much wind either. It ought to be just as warm as anywhere else.'

Further on, towards the head of the valley, what they could glimpse of the woods seemed perfectly normal. The trees there were bathed in warm afternoon sunlight, and coming along the top of the cliffs at the head of the valley they had noticed nothing strange — in fact the valley from there had looked excitingly inviting. But around them here the colours were all wrong — yellows and browns and dowdy golds. More leaves fluttered off the trees as they stood there. A sodden carpet of them had already begun to form on the ground. And it was cold even though they were standing in a patch of sunlight.

The sunlight itself seemed watery.

'Back or forwards?' Daniel asked doubtfully.

'I don't know.'

'You decide,' Daniel said.

'I think we should go on to see how far it goes. Someone ought to find out.'

'Okay,' Daniel nodded grimly. 'It can't do any harm. I hope.'

They started off along the towpath again, gazing about at every step they took and taking stock of what they saw. Two hundred yards later they emerged into a larger clearing that was full of bright and glorious sunlight, and there it was summer even if it had been autumn where they'd just passed through.

There was a wide open space on their side of the canal, a triangular wedge of grass and bushes which ran in among the trees. At the end of the wedge they glimpsed the cottage Daniel had remembered from his previous visit. A path had probably once led to it through the grass, but all traces of it had long since gone. More impressive though — and for the moment it took their minds off what they'd seen — were the sides of the valley. Cliffs surrounded the valley-head. The cliffs fell sheer from the top to the bottom of the valley and overhung it. They looked impossible to scale without climbing gear.

Johnny took his eyes away from them first.

'It's all right here, isn't it?' he said. 'How could it have been so cold back there though?' He turned to look the way they'd come.

'I just don't know,' Daniel said. 'Why should it be autumn there and summer here? I've never heard of a cold patch in the middle of nowhere.'

The autumn effect stopped at the edge of the clearing in which they were standing, but looking towards the cottage they saw autumn colours deeper in the wood. Then Johnny pointed across the canal. 'Look!' he said.

Daniel whistled with surprise.

The trees on the far side of the canal crowded right down to the bank, tall strong trees whose uppermost branches touched to form a canopy. Among them the dividing line between summer and autumn was as clear as could be. One tree almost opposite them was in its glossy summer colours, but the next was an autumn gold; and the next and the next and all the trees beyond it were losing their leaves.

'It's like someone's drawn a line round part of the wood,' Daniel said. 'All the trees inside it have gone wrong.'

'What now?' Johnny asked.

'Let's go and have a look at the canal tunnel, then we'll have another think.'

They did so. The end of the tunnel was a low-arched opening into a face of rock with a lot of darkness behind it. The keystone of the arch had an inscription on it, but it was overgrown with moss and impossible to read. A faint current of air blew out of the tunnel. It was funny to think it had probably come all the way under the hill from Summerfield.

They drifted back towards the autumnal part of the wood. Fifty yards short of it, opposite the cottage, they stopped and looked again.

'I don't know what it's all about,' Daniel said, breaking the silence. 'I can't think of anything to explain it. Let's tell my Dad about it. Maybe he'll know.'

'That's a good idea,' Johnny agreed.

Johnny swept his eye along the valley rim again. He couldn't see a single way up. It was certainly a most closed-in place.

Then Daniel gave Johnny a shock. He grabbed his arm and spun him round to look at the other side of the canal. 'Will you believe it! It's spreading!'

'What is?'

'That tree was all right when we came here first, I swear it.'

'You're imagining it.'

'No, I'm not,' Daniel insisted. 'It's a different kind by itself — the others are beech, and that was the last tree to still have its summer leaves.'

'Are you sure?' Johnny said.

'Yes!'

Johnny was certain in a moment that Daniel was right. The tree was in the very first stages of getting its autumn colours. Not a leaf had fallen from it, but the gloss and sparkle had gone while the next tree to it shone with summer. 'It won't be the only one then,' he said. He swivelled round to look towards the cottage. He was right. The autumn line seemed to have advanced towards them from that direction too, just during the few minutes they'd spent visiting the tunnel entrance.

'It's getting worse and worse,' Daniel said. He began to move down the towpath. 'Dad's not going to believe a word of this.'

Johnny followed Daniel out of the sunlight and in among the trees. Over the line the cold frosted his bare arms. And it seemed gloomier too than it should be, as if dusk had fallen early. The towpath bent, cutting them off completely from the bright sunlight. Suddenly Johnny didn't like it very much. 'Hurry! Hurry!' he found he was saying to himself. A bramble caught in his trouser leg and without realising what it was he struggled frantically to free himself. There was a tearing and rending sound of cloth ripping. He didn't stop to look at the damage.

They passed the little clearing where they'd first noticed the effect and went round the bend that took them to the lock. The trees were still autumnal here and the ground scattered with dead leaves. How had they managed not to have noticed it earlier? Because they'd been running, he supposed. They went down the slope beside the lock. It had taken them five or six minutes fast walking to pass through the part of the valley affected. 'It's all right ahead!' Daniel announced.

Then something stirred in the branches of the trees on their side of the canal. The two boys froze as the noise became louder. Suddenly a creature flew out from above their heads. It was a dark, long-tailed bird.

'A bird!' Daniel couldn't have sounded more relieved.

'That was all!' Johnny echoed faintly. 'I imagined all sorts of things in these few seconds!' He turned to watch the bird glide into the trees on the other side of the canal where it was quickly hidden from view. A moment later it chattered to itself.

The two boys grinnned at one another. 'Noisy thing!' Daniel said and began walking on more briskly. But then something happened to Johnny.

It was as if a very indistinct voice spoke in his head. It was as if he was touching the mind of something or someone with his own mind. He tried to drive the feeling away, but it didn't go.

'Come on,' Daniel called from some way ahead.

Johnny started moving. The feeling got stronger.

'We're out of it,' he heard Daniel saying. 'It stops as abruptly here as at the other end. What's the matter with you?'

Johnny pushed past Daniel. 'Run!' he shouted. 'Run!' What was touching his mind had made a sudden jump that brought it much closer. It was coming through the trees towards them. It would be on them in a minute. He plunged off down the towpath. Daniel glanced around wildly, then followed Johnny.

Johnny didn't stop till he'd reached the lane. There he grabbed Daniel's bike and pushed it into his friend's hands, then grabbed his own.

'What's the matter?' Daniel said.

'Let's get away first,' Johnny replied. He threw a leg over his bike and began pedalling furiously up the lane towards the track back to Summerfield. There had been nothing to see, but something had begun to home in on them during those last few minutes.

Some minutes later they were up on the track and gazing down at the valley from the top of the cliffs. Very peaceful it seemed under the late afternoon sun.

'It was the gloom in there made you panic,' Daniel reasoned with Johnny. Johnny had just explained why he'd run. 'The wood just shouldn't have been like it was, and that must have preyed on your mind more than you realised. Then the bird flew out and startled us. It could have happened to you, me or anyone.'

Johnny wasn't so sure, but his experience had left him too tired to argue.

Daniel began wheeling his bike on up the hill. 'I'll tell Dad all about that autumn part of the wood,' he said, 'and the cold. He'll know what caused it.'

Johnny took one last look at the valley, then hurried after Daniel.

That voice seemed to have been trying to talk to him.

— 4 —

Kaa screamed as his father fell under the wolf . . . Kaa screamed as the wolf's weight crushed him . . .

Johnny jerked awake with a start. For several moments he wasn't sure where he was. The wolf's teeth tore into his own neck. It was he who struggled for his life. Only gradually did the familiar curtains, the knocked about chest-of-drawers and his posters on the walls begin to make sense.

In the dream — for now Johnny knew it had been one — Kaa had been climbing up a rock-face. The wind had nearly blown him off it. Then he'd looked down and heard his father wailing out that the priest's magic necklace was lost. And then he'd seen the wolf leap on him.

Who was Kaa?

Downstairs Johnny heard his mother's and father's voices and another — a man's which he didn't recognise. It was probably one of the neighbours or a friend of Dad's who'd popped in for a cup of tea and a Sunday morning chat. But he didn't bother about that. The gloomy atmosphere of the dream was still upon him. He jumped straight out of bed and quickly pulled the curtains open. In daylight things would seem more normal. Outside the sun shone over Denver and seemed to have been up for hours.

Johnny got back in bed and pulled the sheets up to his neck. It was chilly in the room for the sun hadn't reached his window yet. In his dream Kaa had been cold, too. A biting wind had nearly blown him off the rocks as he'd climbed, and he'd swayed dangerously for a moment before regaining his balance. The moon had shown through the clouds momentarily and the frosted ground had sparkled. But where had he got the name Kaa from, and who was he? And where had Kaa been? On a rocky cliff-face — Johnny knew that. Near the sea then? But there had been no sea when Kaa had looked down, only frosty, bare earth. Johnny tried to remember what Kaa's father had looked like, but he remembered only the ferocity of the wolf springing on him and the intensity of Kaa's fear. That gave no clue. And why had Kaa and his father been so upset about losing a necklace? How could a necklace be magic?

Johnny heard the voices downstairs again and pushed the bedclothes back. It had been the oddest of dreams — almost as if Johnny had been Kaa as long as it had lasted. Then he forgot about it. At the sight of his clothes on the chair he remembered the events over at Yonderley and the fact that he was supposed to be meeting Daniel. The church clock began striking from the front of the house and he stopped only to count its strokes. It was ten and he'd meant to be up at seven. He began to throw his clothes on, putting aside the trousers he'd worn yesterday. The rip he'd got rushing back along the towpath had been quite a bad one.

Mum had noticed it straightaway. 'Your leg!' she'd said. 'Have you hurt yourself?'

Dad had paused to glance at his trousers too as he picked up his car keys from the kitchen table. 'You won't be able to wear those anywhere decent now. You're late, you know. We're going out this evening. Didn't you remember?'

'They're old anyway,' Mum had said. 'Mrs Farley is already in watching the television. Go and say hello to her.'

'We went over to Yonderley on the bikes, — you'll never guess what we saw.' That was as far as Johnny had got.

'Go and say hello to Mrs Farley!' Mum had insisted. 'You know she's giving up her evening to come and look after you. You'll have to tell us what you saw tomorrow, interesting as it may be. Your Dad's in a flap—can't you see?'

As he finished fastening his sandals Johnny hoped Daniel had had better luck telling his mother and father. And he hoped too the visitor would go away soon so he could let his parents know his strange story. In the cold light of another morning the idea of what they'd seen seemed utterly fantastic — yet he and Daniel had certainly not imagined it.

Downstairs he hesitated at the living-room door. The stranger he'd heard earlier was speaking again. He didn't know the voice at all and for some reason he felt suddenly shy about meeting whoever it was. The voice had a faint accent and the speaker seemed very cheerful on purpose as if he was being his most friendly for Mum and Dad. Instead of going in to join the grown-ups Johnny went on into the kitchen, but no one was in there and he felt hungry. He waited a moment hoping Mum had heard him come down, but no one came. There was nothing for it. He would have to go into the living-room and meet the visitor. Why was he being so silly? He had no reason and he was in a hurry. He turned round to go back.

Luckily at that moment the living-room door opened and Mum came in from the hall.

'You're up late,' she said cheerfully. 'It's gone ten already.'

'I heard the clock.'

'Daniel's been and gone more than once.'

'Has he? Why didn't you wake me?'

'We'd hardly got up ourselves the first time — we were back quite late last night — and you needed your sleep. You still look tired out. Weren't you saying that you went over Denver to Yonderley yesterday? Isn't that rather off the beaten track?'

'I better go. I arranged to see Daniel,' Johnny replied, ignoring Mum's comments about Yonderley. 'It's important.' He toyed with telling Mum about the woods here and now, but decided it could keep — it had kept all night — and Daniel was obviously impatient. Perhaps his Dad had come up with an explanation.

'Well you can wait a few more minutes,' Mum said. 'Nothing's that important on a nice day like this. Will toast do you?'

Johnny suddenly remembered why he was stuck out here.

'Who's that in the living-room with you and Dad?' he asked.

Mum put the pieces of bread into the toaster. 'Oh, that's your Dad's Australian cousin. I should have taken you in to meet him straightaway.'

'Australian cousin?'

'Yes, you know. He and Dad occasionally send each other Christmas cards. He sent a present a couple of years ago, — ' she lowered her voice, ' — that horrid little china kangaroo.'

Johnny shook his head. He had no memory of it.

'Well pretend you haven't forgotten,' Mum said. 'He won't like to think we never mention him. I told him it got broken in the post which was why it wasn't on show.' She went on in a lower voice. 'It was a bit odd the way he turned up — '

'Odd?'

'No, surprising I mean,' Mum said. 'He didn't give us a moment's warning. He was waiting last night when we got back. Mrs Farley had let him in. We hadn't the faintest idea who he was until he introduced himself. Of course Dad has never met any of that side of this family. He didn't even have any baggage.'

'Where did he sleep?' Johnny said. 'And is he staying?'

'He slept on the sofa in the front room and how long he's staying, well we hadn't thought that far ahead,' Mum said. 'He can stay, of course, but the house isn't really big enough to put people up conveniently for any length of time.'

Johnny remembered the kangaroo now and how Mum had sent it to school for a rummage sale. He hadn't even known it had been his Dad's cousin's present. Why had he so suddenly come to England and arrived at their house without warning?

'So there you are,' Dad's voice boomed out. He had appeared at the kitchen doorway. 'I thought I heard you.' A stranger was with him. 'Charles, this is Johnny. Johnny, this is my second cousin Charles, Charles Madge.'

Johnny took the hand held out to him. He found himself looking into a very cold pair of grey eyes that seemed to see straight through him from behind steel-rimmed spectacles. Rather confused by the intensity of the gaze, he looked away.

Charles Madge was quite tall, on the thin side, and dressed in a dark-blue suit. His hair was cropped short. He was about Dad's age or younger and very sun-tanned.

'You haven't an ash-tray, have you?' Charles Madge said aside to Mum. Johnny watched as he flicked his cigarette into the ash-tray. The cigarette had a gold tip.

'Johnny's learnt all about Australia at school, haven't you?' Dad bragged without giving Johnny a chance to think. 'Now what's the capital? Do you remember?'

'Melbourne.' Johnny blurted out the first Australian city that came into his head. He was busy observing Charles Madge. Did he always stare at people that hard when he first met them?

'Oh, come on!' Dad said. 'What is it? It's not Melbourne.'

Johnny hurriedly corrected himself. 'I mean Canberra.'

'I'll get your toast ready,' Mum said. 'It won't be a moment, Johnny.'

'I'll tell you all about Australia,' Charles Madge chipped in. It was the first time he'd spoken to Johnny. He smiled too, a much more friendly smile than Johnny would have expected after the first glance.

'You'll enjoy talking to your Uncle Charles — I think that's what you'd better call him,' Dad said to Johnny. 'He's my second or third cousin — I'm not sure what relation that makes him to you.'

'Toast,' Mum said.

'Toast — that's a funny kind of relation,' Dad joked weakly.

Johnny took his plate, then realised Charles Madge had begun nodding in agreement when he'd said Melbourne was the capital of Australia. How strange. Charles Madge of all people should have known it was the wrong answer. He was an Australian. But Johnny didn't have time to think about it properly because Mum asked the question Johnny had wanted to ask.

'In all the excitement of your arriving, you never told us why you've come to England,' she said. 'Are you just on holiday?'

Charles Madge tapped his glasses back onto the bridge of his nose. 'It's a bit of both — holiday and work,' he replied. 'The newspaper I worked for in Australia got bought up by another, and those of us who found ourselves out of a job got a lot of redundancy pay. I thought I'd come to have a look at England and maybe in the meantime have a go at writing a book.'

'What about?' Dad said.

'About England. About coming back to the place in England where one's family originally came from. Lots of families in Australia come from around here you know, and I thought there might be quite a lot of interest in a book like that. I was hoping to find somewhere quiet where I could settle down and write it.'

'Quiet?' Dad pricked up his ears. 'How quiet?'

'Somewhere away from the noise and grime of modern life.'

'Next door,' Dad said.

'Great-Uncle Jim's?' Mum asked, puzzled.

'Yes — why not rent Charles the place? We can still keep it on the market.'

'Oh — ' Mum hesitated. 'Are you sure?'

'We'll talk about it anyway,' Dad said. 'I think it's a good idea. Let's all go and sit down over another coffee and see if we can't fix something up.'

'Great-Uncle Jim's?' Charles Madge asked.

Johnny, who still wanted to be off straightaway even if there was the excitment of his 'Uncle' having arrived, saw his chance as Dad and Charles Madge started to move off towards the front room again, Dad explaining about next door. 'Can I eat my toast on the way down to Daniel's?' he said.

'Well, just this once,' Mum agreed.

He was off before she could change her mind.

'Goodbye, Johnny,' Charles Madge said. He gave Johnny another of those intense gazes. 'And Johnny's your only son?' he heard the Australian asking Mum as he went down the back door step.

Johnny put the two pieces of toast together and ate them double like a sandwich as he ran down the garden path. Then he threw the crusts into the hedge and opened up the garden shed which was on Great-Uncle Jim's side of the fence. Pushed between the handle-bar and the brake-cable of his bike he saw a slip of paper. He pulled it out.

'Come quick,' Daniel's note read. 'Something's happened at the farm.'

Something else! So Daniel hadn't just wanted to tell him his father's explanation. What with dreams and long-lost cousins and yesterday's business at Yonderley Johnny didn't know if he was coming or going. What was this going to turn out to be?

He wheeled his bike out onto the road and sped off down the hill.

5

It was another boiling hot day, though the air was rather sticky and moist. By the time Johnny reached the farm-gate he was running with sweat.

Mr Butler was the first person he saw. He came from behind an open door in the yard to see who'd arrived and waved to Johnny. The two knew each other very well.

'Come to clear up our little mystery?' Mr Butler shouted. 'Daniel's been up the lane half a dozen times to see if you were still in bed. Like a cat on hot bricks he is. Maybe you'll calm him down.'

Johnny propped his bike against the wall and climbed over the gate. 'What's happened then?' he said.

'I won't spoil it for Daniel,' Mr Butler replied cheerfully enough. 'He's around somewhere. He'll tell you.'

Johnny hadn't got further than half-way across the yard before Daniel appeared.

'Where have you been?' he snapped.

'Mum didn't wake me up,' Johnny said. 'It isn't my fault. What's happened? Your Dad said you'd tell me.'

'I've been waiting hours,' Daniel grumbled.

Johnny waited. He knew his friend well enough to know that it he started one of their rare arguments Daniel would never get to the point, though it was difficult to wait to hear what had happened. His mind flashed back to yesterday over at Yonderley, but talking about that would obviously have to wait. Then he remembered his strange dream about Kaa, Kaa's father and the wolf. That would interest Daniel.

'All right, I'll show you,' Daniel said.

'What?'

'Wait. Let me tell the story from the beginning,' Daniel went on. Without explaining why he took Johnny over by the pig-sties. Three enormous sows came pushing against the bars, but for once Johnny didn't pay them any attention.

'What have we come here for?' he asked.

'I'd just got back last night from Denver Hill,' Daniel said. 'You remember — after you wouldn't stay here but went rushing home.'

'Mum and Dad were going out,' Johnny said.

'I heard Dad was in with the cows. I was just going in too when these pigs went wild.' Daniel pointed and two of the pigs came back to the bars hopefully.

'Wild?' Johnny looked puzzled.

'Listen, will you! They began rushing all over the place. They were bumping into the walls and into each other. One of them was climbing onto the back of another to try and climb out! Another was banging against the gate. They were scared to death of something.'

'What?' Johnny said.

Daniel shrugged. 'Then suddenly they all stopped,' he went on. 'They faced round into the middle of the pen, backing into the corners as best they could. They were staring at something and I couldn't tell what. There was nothing there, absolutely nothing I could see. I ran for it, I can tell you!'

'But what was it?' Johnny said, wrinkling up his brow.

'I don't know. I'm just telling you what happened.' He took Johnny's arm and steered him towards the cow-shed. 'I could hear Dad in the cow-shed so I headed that way. I rushed in and Dad put up his head, ready to shout at me, when the same thing happened to the cows that had happened over at the pig-sty. It was like whatever it was had followed me. Some of the cows were loose in the walk-way, and Dad was just finishing off the milking. The loose ones all backed down in a panic to the far end of the shed. One of them knocked Dad over in the rush. There were four cows still in the pens. They all stopped absolutely still. They didn't move a thing except their heads to look back at the walkway. You could see all their eyes moving as if they were following something that was behind them.'

'And?' Johnny said.

'Nothing really.' Daniel frowned and pushed his hair out of his eyes. 'Dad and I froze. We were looking, but we couldn't see anything. Dad got up and tried to shoo the untethered cows away from the pens. At first they wouldn't move. Then all of a sudden they sort of relaxed.'

'As if it had gone?'

'Yes.'

'You didn't *see* anything?'

'No.'

'Not a thing.'

'No.'

'Did you feel anything?'

'What do you mean by feel?'

'Like what I felt down at the canal. When I felt something coming through the trees,' Johnny said excitedly.

Daniel shook his head. 'No I didn't, not a thing. I was scared, but that's different. I wouldn't have known about it except for the animals. Let's talk about it somewhere else though. Just talking about it in here makes me feel all creepy.' He led the way out of the cow-sheds. After all he'd been told Johnny was glad to follow him.

Daniel's Dad was in the yard again. He had the top yard-gate open and was about to get into his Land Rover. 'Heard everything about our ghost then?' he said cheerfully.

'Ghost, Mr Butler?' Johnny asked. 'Do you believe in ghosts?'

Mr Butler considered carefully. 'I don't disbelieve in them,' he said. 'Let's put it this way. There are some stories I've heard that seem true enough to me, and there were ghosts in them.' He looked hard at Johnny. 'They were told by people I trust.'

'Well,' Johnny said, 'Mum and Dad always say they're just

stories or there's some other explanation.' He wasn't so sure himself though, especially now.

'Well I'd like your Mum and Dad to explain what happened here yesterday evening when Daniel got home,' Mr Butler said. He grinned at Johnny. 'Anyway it's not here now. The animals are happy enough. They say it's animals sense strange things first before us human beings. I'm off up Denver for an hour or two to do some work. Enjoy yourselves. But don't go fretting over ghosts now. Most of them don't mean any harm.'

'We'll shut the gate,' Daniel said, taking charge again of Johnny who was wondering over Mr Butler's last remark. That was a real eye-opener, a grown-up believing in ghosts.

'Come on — let's find somewhere to talk,' Daniel said as they watched the Land Rover disappear up the hill.

'Yes,' Johnny replied. He suddenly remembered Kaa and his father again — it was strange how the dream and its sadness kept coming back to him, even though there were far more important things to think of. He opened his mouth to start telling Daniel, but Daniel was talking again.

'I've been thinking a lot about what frightened you down at the canal,' he said.

'You said I was imagining it at the time,' Johnny said, pushing Kaa into the back of his mind once more.

'That was *then*,' Daniel said. 'That patch of autumn wood was wrong enough on its own to make you imagine things, and you said so yourself on the way back. But now — '

'What now?'

'You weren't imagining it, were you? You haven't changed your mind about that?'

Johnny suddenly got a vivid impression of yesterday's experience — touching the mind of something or someone else with his own mind — trying to get away from it, but not managing.

'No,' he said, 'I wasn't imagining it. I'm sure. I wish I wasn't sure, but I am.'

'Well,' Daniel continued carefully, 'maybe it and the ghost here last evening are connected. Maybe it followed us over the hill.'

Twenty minutes later the two boys found Mr Butler in one of the fields that lay near the canal valley. They'd passed his parked Land Rover half a mile further down the slope. He was working with a spade by a ditch.

'Come to help?' he asked as he looked up.

'It's not that, Dad,' Daniel said. 'You remember what I told you about what Johnny and I saw over the other side of Denver yesterday?'

'Of course I do,' Mr Butler said. 'The oddest thing I've heard for ages. I promised I'll go over and have a look as soon as I've time.'

'Johnny and I think the two things are connected,' Daniel went on. 'The ghost at the farm and what we saw at Yonderley. There's something I left out because I wasn't sure of it when I was telling you.'

'And what's that?' Mr Butler said. 'I thought what you said about the cold and the trees losing their leaves was peculiar enough.'

'You tell him,' Daniel prodded Johnny.

As carefully as he could Johnny described everything at Yonderley, starting with the cold patch of wood and how strange they'd found it, finishing with what had happened as they were leaving.

Mr Butler considered. He seemed puzzled. 'And you're sure about this, Johnny? You don't think the wood made you . . . '

'No!' Johnny said. 'It wasn't scarey till then.'

'Maybe the two things are connected,' Mr Butler said. 'So you think what Johnny felt and what the animals sensed are the same?'

'Yes,' Daniel said. 'It followed us.'

Mr Butler thought again. He wasn't totally convinced that Johnny hadn't dreamt it all up, Johnny could tell straightaway. 'Isn't that too much of a coincidence, the two things coming up the same day?' he said.

'I didn't get scared over at the canal because of what happened at the farm,' Johnny said. 'It happened the other way round. And you saw what happened here without knowing what I'd felt at Yonderley.'

'That's very true,' Mr Butler agreed. 'I wasn't doubting your word, it's just that I've been frightened to death in woods myself before now.'

'Dad, couldn't you go over to Yonderley and look at the canal today?' Daniel asked. 'Please.'

'I'm afraid not,' Mr Butler said. He pointed up at the sky. 'You see up there?' The boys looked. The sky was an intense blue and almost cloudless except for some wispy trails of cloud high up. 'Those are bad weather clouds up there. Whatever it's like now, the barometer had dropped a mile this morning and this is the last we've seen of summer weather for a few days. I've got jobs to do I can't put off till after it comes. This piece of digging for instance. I don't want the field below flooded out.'

'Oh Dad!' Daniel begged. 'Just an hour!'

'A quarter of an hour at the most. I could come up as far as the top of the hill. I'd be able to see the autumn trees from up there, wouldn't I?'

'No, you wouldn't,' Johnny said disappointed at the way Mr Butler had taken his part of the story. 'We couldn't as we came back up the track yesterday. They seem to be hidden in a dip.'

'That's that then I'm afraid,' Mr Butler said. 'I'm sorry.' He picked his spade up again. 'Don't be surprised though,' he said before going back to work again, 'if something else doesn't happen before long. These things have a way of happening one after the other.'

'Something else?' Johnny said. 'What?'

'Who am I to know?' Mr Butler said. 'Your guess is as good as mine. Just don't conjure anything too terrifying up!'

'But there'll be some perfectly natural explanation for what happened at the farm last night,' Dad said later that day. He was out in the front garden mowing the lawn. Johnny's new uncle Charles Madge was taking a look round the village. Johnny could see him halted in front of the church gazing up at the tower. 'Something – it could have been an insect or anything like that – upset one of the animals, its fear spread and in a minute you have the whole farm affected. Now doesn't that sound more reasonable than Mr Butler's explanation?'

'But, Dad, Mr Butler says he's heard about several ghosts that he believes in.'

'Now, look, Johnny,' Dad said, 'I know Mr Butler and like and respect him, but if you go on talking that way we'll be back to believing in witches and werewolves and goodness knows what. These things can always be explained even if the explanation's difficult to get at. We haven't gone through thousands of years of history getting ourselves civilised to start believing in magic and witchcraft again. You were going to tell me something about the woods over at Yonderley a couple of minutes ago,' Dad reminded him, trying to make up for having been so unbelieving about the Butler's ghost.

Johnny sighed. He supposed he deserved it for having told Dad on more than one occasion that the house next door was 'spooky'.

Johnny told Dad about the autumn woods, and then how he'd scared himself on the way back to the lane from the canal tunnel entrance, without hinting he thought the farm and the canal were connected. He still believed he'd not imagined it all. But if Mr Butler had doubted him, what reaction would Dad have?

Dad told him a long involved story about how he'd panicked down a country lane in the dark once and thought something hideous was following him. It had turned out to be a cow!

Dad went back into the house to find out if tea was ready. Johnny hoped he'd not left Dad with so strong an impression of Yonderley that he'd stop him going back there. However scarey, he was going to return as soon as possible to find out what was really happening. Dad popped his head out of the door. 'Tea's on the table,' he called. 'Just go and fetch your uncle, will you? And, oh Johnny, let's forget all about ghosts and such things, shall we?'

6

Mr Butler had been quite right. Early that evening it began to rain, and it rained all night. On Monday morning when Johnny looked out of his bedroom window a stream of water was flooding and gurgling down the lane below the house. A sheet of rain was still coming down from the clouds. Denver, the woods and fields and the farm were lost in mist. Whatever mystery there was over at Yonderley, he and Daniel wouldn't be out to investigate it for some time.

'It was a good job you remembered to shut your bedroom window,' Mum remarked at breakfast. 'I completely forgot about it last night.'

'Oh yes,' Johnny said. 'It was lucky.' He tried to look as if what she'd said didn't matter. But it did. The fact was that he'd crept out of bed to close it as soon as Mum had gone down from saying goodnight. He had no intention of sleeping with his window open from now on, even if on hot nights he sweltered to death. If there had been something over at the canal at Yonderley and it had followed Daniel to the farm, it might have followed him too.

'Eat up then,' Mum said. 'You've a bus to catch.'

'Okay, Mum,' Johnny said. He'd been thinking about something else before Mum had reminded him about the window – his dream about Kaa and his father and the wolf. He'd had exactly the same dream this morning as he'd had yesterday. Every detail had been the same – the climbing upwards and the wind nearly pushing him off the cliff – Kaa's father wailing out that he'd lost the wolf necklace – then the wolf pouncing. All the same terror had been there. It had been as real as if it had actually happened.

'Did you hear me?' Mum interrupted his thoughts. 'It's not that I want to get rid of you, it's just that you do seem a bit slow this morning. If you're not looking forward to school, at least you've only got a week to go.'

'Nearly finished, Mum!' Johnny gobbled down his remaining food, then rushed to get his coat on. By the time he was ready Mum was holding the door open for him.

'Where's Uncle Charles?' he called back to Mum through the rain. 'I haven't seen him this morning.'

'Gone into town.'

'What for?'

'To fetch his luggage from the station. He went in with Dad. He'll be home this evening,' Mum shouted. 'You'll see him then. Now hurry.'

Johnny ran up the street towards the bus stop where the bus gave all the signs of being ready to start off. The driver revved his engine when Johnny was ten yards away, making him break into a run. He closed the doors and set off immediately Johnny was inside.

Daniel was keeping a seat for him. 'Cutting it a bit fine, aren't you?' he said as Johnny slipped in beside him.

'I know,' Johnny gasped breathlessly. 'Anything else happened at the farm?'

'Nothing,' Daniel said. 'I'm not sure whether I'm glad or not.'

The bus drove past Johnny's and past the turning to the farm and Yonderley. The windows were steamed up and Daniel rubbed furiously to keep them clear to look out.

'This rain puts paid to us going over to Yonderley tonight, and tomorrow probably. You do agree we ought to go over, don't you?' Johnny said.

'Yes,' Daniel agreed without stopping his rubbing. 'We can't just leave it as it is.'

'I had that dream again,' Johnny went on. 'The one I told you about yesterday on the way up to find your father. I hope I don't go on having it. It's really sad. At this rate I'm going to dread going to sleep.'

'It's only a dream,' Daniel said. 'Now that thing down at the farm – that was something to really keep you awake. It did too last night. I couldn't sleep for thinking of it.'

It rained all day without let. Last weeks of school were bad enough without being cooped up inside, and Johnny was more than usually glad to get on the Summerfield bus at four o'clock. Back home he was surprised to find Dad already there.

'I finished early to give your Uncle Charles a lift back,' Dad explained.

As it happened Charles Madge had had no need of him. He was now the possessor of a brand-new Land Rover, bought in town, and the hall was filling up with luggage he'd fetched in it, all plastered with airline stickers saying Qantas Airlines, Australia. The suitcases and bags might have been full of bricks they were so heavy. There were lots of books in them Charles Madge explained as Johnny helped him to carry the rest in. 'I paid an enormous surcharge on the plane to have them travel with me,' he said to Dad. 'I meant to set myself up in a flat in London, you know, then let you know I was here. It was a real spur of the moment decision coming out to you here on Saturday. I'm glad I did it now.'

'So are we,' Dad said.

Mum had tea ready for when they'd finished lugging things around, and they sat straight down to table.

'This looks very nice,' Charles Madge said surveying the spread. 'But you must stop treating me as a visitor. I must be just an extra member of the family, especially when I move in next door.'

'You're staying then?' Johnny said, his mouth full of food. He'd tucked straight in. He'd heard the three grown ups discussing the question last night but not known they'd come to any decision. Not that it made much difference to Johnny – yesterday Charles Madge had been polite and friendly enough, but they hadn't found much to say to each other. Charles Madge didn't seem used to talking to children.

'Oh yes,' Dad said. 'We arranged the final details just before you got in. Your Uncle Charles will have next door for three months. We'll go over to the solicitor's sometime this week or next to iron out the details.'

'A special member of the family,' Mum added, a little flattered by Charles Madge's praise of her cooking. 'At least until tomorrow. The house should be ready for you to move in then. I did some dusting and tidying up round there this morning just in case, and we can light a fire after tea. It won't be thoroughly aired tomorrow, but we can keep the fire in for a few more days and that should do the trick.'

Charles Madge laughed. 'I'll manage,' he said. 'I'm not marvellous at looking after myself, but I'm as good as the next confirmed bachelor, you know.'

'I'm sure you are,' Mum said.

But Dad looked puzzled. 'Weren't you thinking of getting married last time you wrote? Or is my memory playing me tricks?'

'Pardon?'

There was a hush at the table. Charles Madge seemed very taken aback at what Dad had said. 'Married?' he said. The silence went on long enough for Johnny to stop eating and gaze around at the three grown-ups to wonder what was going on. Then light seemed to dawn all at once. 'Oh that!' Charles Madge smiled. 'I nearly was once. I'd forgotten I told you. It was a mistake telling anyone about that.' He took his glasses off and began polishing them vigorously – they'd got all steamed up.

Mum quickly came to the rescue. 'Perhaps Charles doesn't want to talk about it,' she said. 'These things happen. Come on, Johnny. Get on with your tea.'

Johnny hesitated, then did as he was told. He'd been reminded of Charles Madge nodding when he got the capital of

Australia wrong. Johnny could have sworn Charles Madge had said he'd been nearly married just to shut Dad up, as if his fiancée had never existed. Then, on the other hand, Dad could have imagined it – he was always getting letters from someone or other and perhaps he had mixed Charles Madge up with someone else. Johnny got on with his tea and thought no more of it.

After tea when Charles Madge was out of the room Mum warned Dad to steer clear of the subject. 'It's obviously a delicate matter,' she said. 'It seems to have upset him a lot at one time or another. Perhaps he's tried to get her out of his memory.'

'How was I to know?' Dad protested.

'You weren't, but you do now,' Mum said firmly.

When Charles Madge came back in Johnny went to watch television. The adults talked in the kitchen. Johnny did notice though that their visitor smoked very heavily that evening – perhaps, as Mum said, he had been crossed in love and jogging his memory had really upset him.

It rained all Tuesday, too, but when Johnny looked out of his bedroom window on Wednesday morning the clouds had lifted enough for it to be possible to see nearly to the top of Denver. The rain was lighter and as the bus drew up at the school front gates Johnny saw the first ray of sunshine trying to break through. It was a sign of hope. Johnny said so to Daniel. 'Maybe it'll dry up and I'll be able to come down the farm tomorrow.'

'Probably,' Daniel replied. 'Did you have that dream again?'

'Yes,' Johnny said. 'Exactly the same. It's the fourth time now. I can't say I like it much.' He rather dreaded having to go to sleep to wake up to it.

'I've never heard of anything like it before,' Daniel said, shaking his head.

School started with Assembly as usual. Their class did History before play with Mr Waldron, then after play-time, which they'd had to spend inside, Mrs Braithwaite, the English teacher, told them to write about anything they wanted as long as it was exciting and properly spelt. She had some tidying up to do ready for end of term. Outside the weather was improving even more. It was showers and intervals of intensely bright sunshine now. Going to Yonderley tomorrow would probably be possible.

After some thought Johnny began writing about what he'd seen at Yonderley, except he blew everything up so that the autumn woods covered the whole of Denver. At the centre of it all was a ghostly figure that terrified anyone who set foot in there. But before he'd hardly got into his story the teacher told them to listen. She wanted to read out what one of the girls had already finished.

At first Johnny didn't pay much attention. His head was full of his own story and he wanted to get on with it. In fact Mrs Braithwaite called out to him especially to put his pen down and listen.

'That morning we were tired as well as hungry,' Mrs Braithwaite read out. 'My father and I took turns to keep watch but neither of us slept much. The wolf the God had sent to trouble us after we had worshipped at the Great River, and which had followed us every step back from there, came close to the fire that night for the first time. Twice in the night I was woken by my father's cries as he drove it off. Once he had to use his spear and he must have caught the wolf a glancing blow for there was blood on the spear tip when I fetched it back.

'At first light we ate what we could spare from our dried food. It was precious little and left our stomachs feeling even emptier than before. Then my father said the prayers it is necessary for the priest of the wolf-clan to say on the fifth day of the return from the Sacred Journey to the Great River. I listened, learning them as I was supposed to. Afterwards we set off. My father was in a sombre mood. After a time he told me why. He had dreamed during my watch. This was to be the last journey he would make. When it became necessary in seven years' time for the priest to make the journey north again it would be I not he who made it. I said nothing, knowing in my heart that what he said was true. The God tells him the future which is why he is the priest. Later he told me the wolf had also been a sign. Since we are of the wolf-clan it is only right the wolves take an interest in us, but never before, my father said, had a wolf attacked a priest on the Sacred Journey.

'We were among hills now. They were barren and waste like the plain we had left behind. A little grass grew, but mostly the ground was wet and spongy for here it does little but rain and in the winter, which we were at the start of, snow. The sun broke through the clouds once and ahead of us across several other hill-tops we saw the shadow of the first woods on a high hill. It was our destination that night, for on the far side of that hill is a cave where the priest and his assistant on the Sacred Journey must always stay, as the priests and assistants for generations before them have always stayed. The sight of the woods made me cheerful for it meant we were nearing the fringes of the lands where people live, but my father grew more sad still. I understand now why. He knew then the place and manner of his death and had not told me.

'As if time was suddenly short my father began to tell me many things that as a future priest I must know. Particularly he told me about the journey to the Sacred River. He said that many generations ago our people had lived on its banks but that the God had sent ice and snow from the north. After many years the herds of animals moved south and our crops would no longer grow in the bitter cold. Great mountains of ice began to move towards our homes. The forests died tree by tree. Our people moved half a moon's travel to the south, stopping at the places he and I had camped at. Since then every seven years the priest of the wolf-clan had made the journey to the Sacred River. Now the mountains of ice had gone, but the land was still not fit for man or beast to live in. Yet one day our people would go back. It was the God's promise to us and the reason why we must journey so every seventh year. He told me great stories of priests who had battled through the ice and snow to reach their destination. He also told me of the way the priest becomes the priest. He must fight his first wolf wearing the priestly necklace, and kill the wolf cleanly in a fair fight, then take its claws. This necklace of claws is the sign of our priest and it holds the claws of the wolf each succeeding priest has killed. Without it the priest is powerless. Without it – though my father never said so, the thought is unspeakable – people say our tribe will disperse and die.

'As the light began to fade we came over the brow of another hill and saw in front of us a higher and longer hill covered with a wood of pine. It was the hill we had seen from afar. My step quickened though my father was tired and lagged behind. I noticed as I turned to encourage him that the thong of leather on which the wolf's claws are threaded was hanging by a thread from his neck. I said so, but he must have been too deep in thought to have taken any notice.

'We went down the bare hill and up into the wood. There was a faint pathway among the trees. The light was fading faster and faster so we hurried. Then behind us, though far off, we heard the wolf howl. Now we ran, ignoring the path. We arrived at the top of the hill, a bare place of no trees. From it we could have looked back over all the day's journey, but we didn't linger. The wolf was behind us. We plunged down the other side of the hill among the trees. There were trees ahead of us too on the other side of the valley we were going down into. My father called urgently to me to bear right and take care. Suddenly I was on top of a cliff of loose earth and stones, at the head of a little valley that cut into the hillside and lay dusky below me. It was protected all round by cliffs. Its bottom was full of trees.

'My father caught me up. "We are not far from the cave," he said. "We must follow the head of the valley round and there is a safe way down." I followed him now, instead of leading. On the opposite side of the valley he cast around a moment, satisfying himself that this was indeed the spot, then lowered himself over the side. I followed him. It would have been impossible to have climbed down there the first time on my own, but with my father ahead of me it was easy. He guided every foot and handhold. The cave he had spoken of was half-way down the cliff, just below a shelf of rock.

'Later my father sent me to the top of the cliff again to gather some bitter blackberries we had seen there. It is part of the ritual of the priest's assistant. He went on down into the bottom of the valley by way of a spur of rock to find firewood. It was barely possible to see now in the encroaching darkness.

'As I neared the top the wind caught me and I swayed. Then I heard my father running back towards the foot of the cliff calling out, "It is lost! It is lost!" I knew at once what he meant. I looked down in horror, but what I saw was even more horrifying at that moment than the thought of what he had lost. I could see what he could not – the wolf crouching in wait, a lighter blur in the half-darkness.

'I called out but it was no use. The wolf leapt upon him.'

At school the class waited.

'Why did you finish your story there, Lisa?' Mrs Braithwaite said. 'Hasn't it an end? What happened after the wolf jumped?'

Johnny's hand had been in the air from the moment Lisa had mentioned the wolf claw necklace. What he had dreamt four nights now was part of Lisa's story!

7

'I didn't know the end, Miss,' Lisa Masters the writer, a girl from the other end of Summerfield, said. She was red-faced because her story had been read out. 'I don't know.' She hid her face in embarrassment.

Johnny waved his hand even more urgently, then was surprised to see that at least a dozen other children were also waving theirs.

'What is it?' Mrs Braithwaite said. 'Lisa – that story of yours was really very interesting, and amazingly grown up too the way it was written. Only it left an awful lot of questions unanswered. Not only what happened after the wolf leapt, but what the boy's name was. And what had the father lost? It sounded very important to him. Why didn't you say what it was?'

Johnny could answer both these questions. He waved his hand more urgently still. The boy's name was Kaa and what he'd lost that was so important was the wolf claw necklace!

'Yes, what have you all to say?' Mrs Braithwaite said to the waving hands.

'That's our story,' a dozen voices shouted out before Johnny could open his mouth.

'Your story? What do you mean – everyone's!' Mrs Braithwaite said. 'No, one of you speak at a time.'

'That's the story I wrote,' a boy sitting near Johnny said. He was another from Summerfield. Johnny looked round at the hands, noticing something – all the children who had them up were from Summerfield or nearby. Daniel had his hand up too.

'Yes, yes. We wrote the same story too,' children scattered all over the room called out. 'We wrote about the boy and his father and the wolf that was following them.'

'All of you? How could that be?' Mrs Braithwaite said in bewilderment.

The children involved began to look very confused when they realised how many of them there were. As for Mrs Braithwaite, she was speechless for a moment.

'Bring the books out here,' she said at last. 'This is amazing.' There was a rush for her desk. The books were placed open on it. She began to glance through them. 'Yes, Johnny?' she said, looking up as the other children filed back to their places. 'Have you written the same too?'

Johnny suddenly realised he'd left his hand in the air. He let it drop. 'Er, nothing, Mrs Braithwaite,' he said. 'It doesn't matter.'

Lisa had written about his dream. She had given him information that began to make sense of it. The other children had written about it too, but none of them had said they'd dreamt it. Then he realised he'd dreamt it four times now but despite that he still hadn't written about it. Why should that be? Why had he acted differently from all the other children? And why did they all come from Summerfield?

Mrs Braithwaite looked through the books more carefully. She shook her head. 'They're almost all exactly the same,' she said. 'Except of course for some of the spelling. You can't have copied off each other – you sit scattered all over the room. And the writing's so adult. You haven't all been watching the same television programme, have you?' she said as she thought of that.

'No,' everyone replied.

Johnny stared across at his friend, Daniel, but he didn't even glance Johnny's way. He looked as mystified as the rest.

Mrs Braithwaite sighed. 'I'm afraid I don't know what to say,' she said. 'Your stories seem to be about rather primitive people, stone-age people perhaps. What the father told his son sounds just like a description of the Ice Age. You haven't been having lessons about the Ice Age with Mr Waldron, have you?' Mrs Braithwaite asked, her face brightening at the thought of another easy explanation.

'No,' the children said.

'It's impossible! How could you all know so much about a period like that? Now, don't all call out at once,' she said, 'but, Lisa, tell me – when you started writing this story, when did you mean to set it?'

'I really don't know, Miss.' Lisa tried to explain. 'It sort of wrote itself. I didn't have to think about it.'

'Wrote itself?' Mrs Braithwaite said.

'Yes, Miss,' the others chorused. 'We found that too.'

'They either all banded together to make a joke, or there's some sort of spooky explanation,' a boy at the front table who'd not written the story called out. 'I read once about something called Automatic Writing. A ghost or spirit is supposed to guide the hand of whoever's writing.'

A shiver went through the room.

Johnny stood up and called out himself at that. Usually he kept pretty quiet in class, but this time he felt he had to say something. 'Mrs Braithwaite,' he called. 'I know the boy in the story's name – it's Kaa. And the thing his father had lost was the wolf claw necklace.'

'And how do you know that, Johnny?'

'I've dreamt I was this boy, Kaa, since Saturday night, every night. I really have. Everything Lisa's story said fits in with my dream.'

There was a gasp from the class.

Mrs Braithwaite put her hand up for silence. 'It does?' she said. 'Oh, this is beyond me, it really is. There seem to be powerful psychic forces at work here. It does sound like automatic writing. That would account for everyone's stories being written in such a grown-up way.'

'Psychic? What's that?' someone said.

Mrs Braithwaite wrote the word up on the board. P–S–Y–C–H–I–C. 'It means "to do with the mind". The things that produce ghosts, or make some people able to communicate with the dead – or say they do. Oh dear, I don't know what your parents are going to say when they hear about this. I think we'd better forget all about it for the moment.'

'What's this all about?' Daniel said a quarter of an hour later, grabbing Johnny's arm on the way out to dinner. 'I don't know how I came to write that story – like Lisa said, it wrote itself – but, do you know, I didn't even think of your dream till you mentioned it in class.'

Only Mum was in when Johnny got home. Dad was working to his usual time and Mum said Charles Madge had been in town all day at the library researching for his book. She didn't know when to expect him.

Johnny mooched about. There was nothing on the television he wanted to watch, and the weather was drizzly again. He tried asking, but the answer was a foregone conclusion. 'You can go down Daniel's, tomorrow,' Mum said, 'when it's stopped raining altogether. Cheer up. The long-range forecast is good — just right for your holiday.'

From the kitchen window Johnny traced the path he and Daniel had taken over Denver last Saturday, but he was thinking mostly of Kaa and the stories about him. He and Daniel and the others had talked about nothing else since dinner, but no one was any the wiser for all their talk. Even the Headmaster had come into their class this afternoon bent on getting to the bottom of it, but despite all his questions, he hadn't made head or tail of it either. Johnny still needed to talk about it so he told Mum. At first she had the usual doubts — thinking some of the children had got together to trick the teacher — but when she heard how seriously Mrs Braithwaite and the Headmaster had taken it, she made him repeat the story all over again. 'Extraordinary!' she said. 'You must tell Dad when he comes in.'

'He'll never believe me,' Johnny said. 'You know what he's like about ghosts and those kinds of thing, and, this is a ghostly thing — psychic Mrs Braithwaite called it.'

'I know what Dad's like,' Mum said, 'but he'll be interested all the same, if only to prove that it could never have happened. But this seems so authentic.'

'Authentic?' Johnny looked puzzled.

'Like it's really happened.'

'But it did!' Johnny pleaded. 'Why is Dad so dead set against ghosts?'

'Oh it's just the way he was brought up,' Mum said. 'He just believes everything can be explained without believing in things you can't see. I tend to agree with him, though in this case . . .' She shook her head.

The wood over at Yonderley might be explained that way, Johnny thought. But not the other strange things he'd got involved in recently.

'Here's your Uncle Charles,' Mum said, glancing out of the window. 'He's had a long day at the library. Work gone well?' she said as he knocked and came in.

'Reasonably,' he said cheerfully. 'Hello, Johnny.'

Johnny chanced to glance at Charles Madge's feet. His shoes were clean but his trousers were caked with mud around his knees.

Charles Madge followed his glance. 'Damn!' he said. 'I changed my shoes but I forgot the trousers. How silly can you get?'

'How did it happen?' Mum asked.

'As I was driving back I heard a rattle in the back of the Land Rover. I pulled up on the verge to find out what it was and stepped right into this lot.'

'It's still sopping,' Mum said. 'You'd better go and get changed now while I'm making tea,'

'I'm going upstairs,' Johnny said when Mum had given him his cup of tea.

'You've no need to,' Mum said.

'I want to think about Kaa.'

From his bedroom he could hear Mum and Charles Madge laughing and talking below. Later Dad drove up and his voice joined the conversation. This only distracted him from thinking. Kaa would have become priest if his father had died. Had Kaa found the necklace? Had he become priest? If he hadn't found it, what had Kaa said would happen — that his tribe would die and the people disperse? He felt a kind of friendship towards Kaa even if he was only a boy in a dream. Kaa must have been about the same age as Johnny himself. What a different kind of life he must have led, a boy in the Ice Age!

Then Johnny laughed. He was thinking of Kaa as if he'd really existed.

Perhaps he had.

'But why should Johnny have had the dream and more than once at that — and the other children not dreamt it, but written the story?' Dad said after tea. 'I must admit I'm usually dubious about stories like this — they leave me cold. I just know there must be some logical explanation. But assuming that the children weren't playing some kind of trick — which we know they weren't because Johnny had already had his dream — how did all those children come to write the same story? The chances against that happening and Johnny's dream being the same must be enormous — millions and millions to one. I wonder if this is the last we've heard of it — Johnny, you must tell us if anything else comes up.'

'I will, Dad,' Johnny said, wondering whether it was the right moment to reintroduce the story of the ghost at the farm and even tell Dad more about what had happened on Saturday afternoon. He decided not to because Charles Madge was there.

'Yes, you must tell us, Johnny,' Charles Madge said. He'd not said a word all through the story; nor had he said anything about Dad's comments after it. But he'd followed what had been said surprisingly closely.

'Ghosts!' Dad continued. 'There are lots of stories about them round here. Do they interest you, Charles?'

'Oh, reasonably,' Charles Madge said. 'I expect to have a chapter in my book about them.'

'I thought you were writing about facts!' Dad laughed.

Later that evening Mum sent Johnny next door with a pair of slippers Charles Madge had left behind. It was getting dark, near bedtime. Johnny stepped over the fence that separated the two gardens and walked to Madge's back door. He glanced over to Denver as he did so and noticed that in one of the fields the sheep were moving around rather restlessly. In the dusk it was impossible to see why. Perhaps a fox was passing by, he thought. He knocked at the door. 'Come in,' Charles Madge called. 'Ah, it's you, Johnny — ' he said as Johnny came through the kitchen into the living-room.

'Mum sent your slippers,' Johnny said and was ready to be off. However Charles Madge quickly got up from the table, where he appeared to have been arranging some books, and came round it.

'Don't go straightaway,' he said. 'Come and sit down for a minute. Let's have a chat. We haven't really got to know each other yet.' He pointed Johnny to a chair next to the roaring fire Mum had lit on Monday evening and not let go out since. He sat down opposite Johnny.

'Chat? What about?' Johnny asked, not quite sure he wanted to, but not wishing to seem impolite.

'Oh anything.' Charles Madge shrugged his shoulders. 'There are lots of things. For instance, is that your bike that's kept in the shed at the bottom of my garden?'

'You won't mind me keeping it there still, will you?' Johnny asked anxiously, thinking he might want the shed cleared out for some reason or other.

'No, why should I? I won't be using the shed, not as far as I know anyway. Do you keep it there for a special reason?'

'Yes,' Johnny said. 'Through the back gate's a short-cut when I go to my friend, Daniel's.'

'And where does Daniel live?'

'Down the lane, then up Denver a bit, on the farm — his Dad owns it.'

'And do you and Daniel go anywhere special on your bikes?'

Charles Madge asked.

For a split second Johnny imagined Charles Madge had somewhere definite in mind, for he gave Johnny another of those quick penetrating looks Johnny had noticed before.

'How do you mean?' Johnny said in a puzzled way.

'Well, you know around here better than me,' Charles Madge grinned, 'in fact I don't know round here at all well.'

'Daniel and I go up the fields on Denver a lot,' Johnny said, 'though bikes aren't much use up there. Is that where you mean?'

'That's the hill the backs of these houses face, isn't it?'

'Yes,' Johnny said.

'With Yonderley on the other side?'

'Yes.'

'It is a rather massive and lonely looking hill,' Charles Madge went on, 'and Yonderley — "yonder" — "over there" — is an even more lonely kind of name. I must visit it some day. Have you been?'

'No, not to the village,' Johnny said.

'Oh.' Charles Madge got up from the chair. 'I fancy some orange or lemon. What about you?'

'Orange, please,' Johnny said. 'But don't bother.'

'No bother. We're having such an interesting conversation.'

Charles Madge went out. Johnny looked round to see what changes had been made in the room. Three of the arm-chairs Great-Uncle Jim had had were gone, but otherwise things were much the same except for the writing-desk that had been brought in from the front room. On it stood a large, new-looking electric typewriter. The other main change was the bookcase behind the writing-desk which had five shelves of books, some with library markings on the spines, but mostly old-looking books that must be the ones Johnny had helped carry in. Then Johnny noticed a stange-looking gadget on the socket the typewriter was plugged into. He was just about to get up and investigate when Charles Madge came in with two glasses.

'Orange for you and lemon for me.' He held out a glass. 'So

you don't always have adventures like this morning's at school?'

'No,' Johnny said. Again he got the impression that his cousin was looking for a definite answer. He looked even more puzzled at him. What kind of answer could he want?

'I mean, have you ever had anything similar happen to you?'

Johnny shook his head. 'No.'

'What I wonder is where your dream — your recurring dream — comes from.'

'Comes from?'

'What caused it, then.' Charles Madge said patiently. 'I mean —you're still having the dream, aren't you? And the stories that were in the children's minds too. All dreams come from somewhere, you know. Generally it's your sleeping mind thinking about things that have gone on during the last twenty-four hours. But this seems different. Could a special place or something you did or saw have caused it, and the children's stories too?'

'Something special?' Johnny said slowly. An idea was dawning on him. 'Or somewhere *I* might have gone?'

'Yes,' Charles Madge agreed quickly. He waited a split second. 'Any ideas?'

'Yes,' Johnny said excitedly. The wood at Yonderley — the mind he'd touched — the ghost at the farm. He told Charles Madge everything and his cousin sat absorbed in every word, so absorbed that he let one of his gold-tipped cigarettes burn down to his fingers.

When Johnny had finished Charles Madge said, 'You must tell me about anything else strange that happens to you. Who knows — after I've finished this book I might turn novelist and make a story out of what you've told me!'

'Yes,' Johnny murmured, but he was in a daze going over the idea that his cousin had given him — that Kaa and Yonderley might be connected.

—8—

'I don't see how they could all be connected,' Daniel objected on the bus next morning. 'They're all so different. In any case the rest of the class hasn't been over to Yonderley.'

'He didn't say they *were* connected,' Johnny said. 'He didn't even say they might be. There's a difference. A suggestion — no, not even that. I worked it out for myself. What he said just put the idea into my head, that's all. He started talking about something altogether different after.'

'We don't even know the ghost at the farm's connected with Yonderley,' Daniel went on, 'let alone with the stories we wrote yesterday. Dad's full of stories about ghosts that hang about farms — boggarts he calls them. He doesn't seem to think that what happened at the farm's anything really out of the ordinary.'

'I know, I know,' Johnny said in exasperation. 'That's not the point.'

'What is the point?'

'I want to find out if they are connected,' Johnny said, 'and to do that we need to go back to Yonderley.' He paused a moment. 'Will you still come?'

'I'm not chickening out,' Daniel said.

'Tonight after school then,' Johnny suggested. 'Okay?'

'I don't like it, but yes,' Daniel said.

They left it at that. It was the way they both felt, more than a little apprehensive.

Johnny rushed home through the sunshine that afternoon. Charles Madge's Land Rover wasn't outside, though Dad's car was. Johnny couldn't imagine why at this time of the day.

'I'm going to Daniel's,' he shouted to Mum as he dumped his satchel off in the hall. He rushed upstairs and changed his uniform for older clothes. Back downstairs he pulled on his wellingtons out in the porch. 'Half past six,' Mum called out. 'At the latest.'

'Is Uncle Charles at the library as usual?' Johnny said. He wouldn't have minded telling him where he was going, just so someone in the house knew — but there was no real need. What possible danger could he be in?

'Yes, he is,' Mum replied. 'He prefers to work in there during the day, though I'd have thought it was quiet enough next door. He says the only time he leaves it is for a bite at lunch time. Where are you going?'

'Just up on Denver.'

'I'm going over the other side of Denver,' Dad's voice said. 'Forgotten me, have you?'

Johnny jumped. 'You're back early, Dad,' he said. 'Why are you going over there?'

'An errand of mercy,' Dad explained. 'One of the men in the office has just moved into a house over near Yonderley — really isolated it is — and he's gone down with flu. We thought he could do with a bit of help — he's not got a thing fixed up in the house yet.'

'Yonderley?' Johnny said. Just where he and Daniel wanted to go.

'Fancy coming?' Dad said.

'Yes please,' Johnny answered hurriedly. 'Could we pick Daniel up on the way?' They would have to be careful though not to let slip their purpose in going over there.

'The more the merrier,' Dad said. 'You look perfectly ready with those wellingtons on. Come on, then.'

Ten minutes later they were driving into Yonderley. It wasn't really big enough to call a village. There were half a dozen sleepy-looking cottages close together and a telephone box, but nothing else — not even a shop or pub.

Dad drove through the village and out the other side. Johnny was glad to see that he must be taking them quite close to the canal. When they were out of sight of the cottages Dad drew up and got out of his breast pocket a rough map which he'd sketched on the back of an envelope. He studied it. 'Where I'm going must be round the next corner according to this,' he mumbled. He glanced round at the view. 'It's marvellously quiet out here, isn't it? It makes Summerfield seem like a busy town. What are you two going to do? Wait for me?'

'You drop us off where you're going, then we'll meet you back there,' Johnny said immediately. 'We'll do some exploring.'

Dad drove the car round the corner and parked it on the verge in front of a bungalow. It was in the middle of a field. The woods Johnny and Daniel had come down through on Saturday afternoon stood above it on the hill. Johnny had the door open before Dad had switched the ignition off.

' 'Bye, Dad!' he shouted. 'Come on, Daniel.'

The lane kept to the same contour along the hillside, and the woods crept down to meet it. After a couple of bends they reached the point where the track came through the woods. The lane dipped down. They stopped and had their first sight of the canal valley.

'It's spread,' Daniel said straight away. 'You can see the autumn colours from the road now. You couldn't before, definitely.'

But it was something else that had caught Johnny's eye. They weren't the only people there. Below them, by the bridge over the canal, a vehicle was parked, a Land Rover. Johnny pointed. 'Someone else,' he said. 'Have they found it too?'

Daniel shaded his eyes and gazed. 'Maybe it's someone out shooting,' he replied. 'Come on. This hanging-about is making me nervous. That thing at the farm may not have hurt Dad and me or the animals, but it was pretty frightening, I'm telling you.

And if it was the same thing you felt . . .'

'I'm nervous too,' Johnny said. 'But you're right. Let's not hang about.'

He had only gone a few yards further, however, when he gasped with surprise.

'That's my Australian cousin's Land Rover,' he said.

'Your Uncle Charles?' Daniel said. 'What's he doing here?'

'I can't think,' Johnny said.

'Well, come on.' Daniel urged him on. 'He's probably having a look after what you told him. I can't say I mind having an adult around here either.'

'No, wait,' Johnny grabbed Daniel's jacket. His mind was doing overtime. 'Let's stay here a moment.'

'Why?' Daniel said.

'He told Mum he was spending the day in the library,' Johnny said. 'What's he doing here?'

'He may be on his way home.'

'Yes, but . . .'

'But what?'

'I don't like it,' Johnny said. 'He didn't take a scrap of notice of me except the odd stare till yesterday tea-time when I told Dad about the stories at school. He didn't say anything in front of Mum and Dad, but the moment he had me on his own — I told you about the conversation we had — he got all the information he could out of me, —'

'He is writing a book about round here, isn't he? Maybe he's come to get information for it. That's the explanation,' Daniel said.

'I don't trust it,' Johnny said decisively. 'I don't know why but I don't want to go rushing down. I just have a feeling about him. I had it when I first met him and I've got it now. Let's wait here till he comes back to the Land Rover, then decide whether we should go and speak to him or not.'

Daniel grumbled, but there was a convenient gap in the bushes from which they could still see the bridge and the Land Rover. They pushed into it, and crouched down, though Daniel continued to complain.

Charles Madge didn't keep them waiting for long. They had hardly settled down before he appeared on the end of the towpath and was at the back door of his Land Rover bundling something in. His tall figure straightened up. He glanced quickly round, then went to the driver's door.

'What was he carrying?' Daniel whispered.

'It looked like a small pick-axe. But he had a spade as well.'

'I saw that,' Daniel said. 'He's been digging. What for?'

'Search me,' Johnny shrugged. 'I don't know what he's up to. I know he's never, ever mentioned anything about having to come over here. In fact he was going on the other night at tea about how he ought to explore some of these back roads. He told me last night he'd never been to Yonderley. But he's been over here before today. It's obvious.' He felt quite distressed at the way Charles Madge had handled him last night.

'How can you tell?' Daniel said.

'Didn't you notice? He was smothered in sweaters. This isn't the first time he's been here if he came prepared for the cold. Last night I didn't tell him anything about how cold it was. It must be still colder in there if he needs to be that dressed up. So he must have known before he came. And I didn't tell him anything that would have meant him bringing pick axes and spades.'

Charles Madge drove off. His Land Rover passed out of sight in the opposite direction from them.

'He knew everything already last night,' Johnny said. 'He was deceiving me and leading me on. He only wanted to find out what I knew and who else knew.'

'But why? Why's it so important to him?' Daniel asked in bewilderment.

'Let's go and find out,' Johnny said grimly, jumping back into the road. 'I really want to know now. I *need* to know!'

9

'He must have been in there for some time so it must be safe for us,' Johnny said, setting off quickly down the road. He didn't know what to think about his cousin's deception. He could see no point to it. 'We'll find where he was digging,' he added.

'Digging for what?' Daniel asked.

'We'll find out,' Johnny replied, ignoring the nervous way his tummy was churning about.

They reached the bridge and turned onto the towpath, immediately walking out of the sunlight as they passed among the trees. Johnny tried to put out of his mind his fears of something or someone strange coming through the woods. Charles Madge had come to no harm, had he? Why should they? In fact Charles Madge hadn't looked scared at all. He'd just calmly loaded the Land Rover and driven off as if he'd done it many times before. Why had he driven off in that direction though? It would be much further to get home that way. Was it so he could come home by way of the road from town and so arrive back the way they all expected him?

They were approaching the first bend of the canal now and they felt the cold already.

'It's moved,' Daniel whispered. 'I wasn't just imagining it.'

'What has?' Johnny started at his friend's voice.

'You were miles away,' Daniel continued. 'The world could blow up sometimes without you noticing! Whatever's wrong around here has moved, hasn't it? It's practically at the lane.'

They were at the first bend of the canal now and already they were among autumn trees. Daniel pointed ahead through the gloom. 'That's where it had got to last time, just before the lock. It's travelled several hundred yards since we were here last.' There was an icy haze on a puddle they had to step around. 'Your cousin, whatever he's up to, was sensible to come well-wrapped up.'

'Yes, Johnny said without listening properly. Fearfully he was opening his mind, trying to detect the thing that had touched it last time. But nothing. There was no trace. He was certain of that. It was a relief — even though it was the reason why he'd come. 'Come on,' he said to Daniel, taking charge and pushing past him on towards the lock.

'I hope it *is* harmless,' Daniel said, following.

'His trouser legs were soaked with mud around the knees when he came in yesterday,' Johnny said. 'The mud must have splashed above his wellingtons when he was down here. I bet he's not been near the library more than once.'

Then suddenly, and he was totally unprepared for it, Johnny got that feeling he'd had last time. Something was touching his mind, very very faintly, something strangely familiar, not just from his previous experience over here but from somewhere else. He pulled up sharply.

'What have you stopped for?' Daniel said, suddenly crowding up behind him.

'I had that feeling again.'

'You did?' Daniel looked around in alarm. 'Are you sure?'

'It's gone,' Johnny said. 'Your talking — I couldn't concentrate.'

'You're probably imagining it,' Daniel whispered nervously. 'You're on edge. So am I. It was just a scare. Let's push on. It's creepy enough without imagining things. We only meant to have a look, remember, not go all the way in.'

'I didn't imagine it,' Johnny said. There had been something familiar about what had touched his mind. But what could it be? It was almost like having seen a person's face he knew, but couldn't put a name to. A person, though? How could a person he knew be out here?

They moved on up the slope past the lock into the area of the wood where they'd first noticed things were wrong, and here things were so different they stopped short, taken aback. Johnny's recent experience was driven right out of his mind. Everything was dead or dying. Leaves had fallen from trees and bushes and they lay in dark heaps on the ground; even the trees seemed to be diseased. Twigs, branches and trunks were a frightening deathly black, mottled here and there with unhealthy silver flecks.

Johnny involuntarily moved closer to Daniel.

A gust of wind blew through the trees, an icy gust that made them shiver from head to toe in their summer clothes, and down from the trees came dead twigs that rattled against the branches. Then there was a silence in which nothing moved at all, and as Johnny gazed stealthily around he found he was being watched by two bright eyes from a fallen branch under the nearest tree. It was a bird, its feathers puffed up to protect it from the cold.

'It's winter here,' Daniel said excitedly. 'That's what's wrong. Dead of winter. All that's missing is snow. Those trees have been crippled by frost — but frost that severe this time of the year! Look, it's practically killed them. Trees that tall and strong!'

The two ventured on. The further they went the colder it became. It was a mid-winter wood now, not just an autumn one. The ankle-deep leaves rustled as they walked and their depth muffled the steps they took. Johnny gazed up past the gaunt tree-tops to the sky above. It was an intense blue but it was cold, whereas on the road and at the bridge it had been a warm inviting colour.

They passed the next bend and the little clearing where Johnny had tasted the blackberries last time. The brambles were dead, beaten into the ground by rain, and a large icy puddle occupied most of the clearing. They side-stepped it and pushed on towards the next clearing from which they would be able to see the cottage. Soon they were there.

Here everything had been normal before. Now it was like the worst part of the wood. The destruction the cold had wrought spread onwards to the tunnel entrance and they could see it clearly through the bare trees now. Looking up, Johnny and Daniel saw that autumn and winter had even climbed out of the valley and onto the hillside above.

'It seems to be spreading faster onto the hill towards Summerfield than towards Yonderley and the road,' Daniel observed, but Johnny didn't answer. He just stood and wondered.

Then Daniel noticed another thing. 'Your Australian cousin!' he said. 'He's definitely been here more than once. You were absolutely right. He's beaten a path from here to the cottage. Look — that wasn't here before.'

There was a well-trodden path from the towpath to the cottage.

'That's the way we go then,' Johnny said, snapping out of it. He stepped onto Charles Madge's path. 'Maybe now we'll find some answers to our questions.'

Johnny scrambled first over the wall round the cottage. The cottage was close through the trees. Not a leaf was left on the branches or the bushes except for an odd dead one that fluttered madly in the gusty wind.

'The cottage's in ruins,' Daniel said. 'It's even more ramshackle than I remember.'

Not one window had its pane of glass in. There was a gaping hole in the roof where it looked as if the chimney-stack had fallen through.

'What are we after?' Daniel said as they carefully stepped towards the low front door. Johnny didn't answer. 'You didn't look very happy back there when you thought you could hear something,' Daniel said. 'You quite worried me.'

'I know,' Johnny said. 'But I think that was my mind going all scarey and making things up. Oh, I don't know. I wish I did. You know, I think I probably did hear something, though “hear” is the wrong word. It was more like a voice in my head. I told you how confusing it was the first time we came.’

They had reached the doorway to the cottage. The door was off its hinges, half-buried in the earth beside the path which had long ago cracked and been broken up into crazy paving by the grass. But the route Charles Madge had taken suddenly became obvious. He had beaten another path which avoided the cottage altogether and went round the back of it.

‘Come on,’ Johnny said. ‘We’ll follow his path. No point in looking in the cottage. I wonder where he goes.’

Daniel shrugged. ‘Somewhere definite anyway. He looks very organised. This disease or cold or whatever it is is spreading, isn’t it? Maybe he found out where it was spreading from and what started it.’

‘Maybe that’s what we’re going to find out,’ Johnny said. ‘I wonder if it’s got anything to do with my “voice”.’

The path took them through the smaller trees that had sprung up in the garden since it had been abandoned, over a dry-stone wall that Charles Madge seemed to have broken down in impatience, and back into the main part of the wood. There was a smell of decay here, of rotten wood. Whole great branches had fallen to the ground. The cold took away their breath.

‘The cold’s getting worse each step we take,’ Johnny said. ‘I’m sure it is.’ A nasty thought suddenly struck him. ‘What if it doesn’t stop spreading?’

‘What?’ Daniel said.

‘What if this doesn’t stop when it’s killed everything down the canal? What if it keeps going? This disease or whatever it is. It must be a disease, mustn’t it?’

‘Perhaps it’s just the cold,’ Daniel said. ‘And I don’t know what the answer to your question about spreading is. Perhaps it will just peter out, like a stone’s ripples in water. But it shows no signs of doing that, does it?’

The path took them out of the trees altogether onto rising ground below the cliffs and then faded away. It was rocky from here on, massive boulders piled one on top of the other, higher and higher, until eventually they were piled half-way up against the cliff-face. For a moment Johnny imagined they were looking in from some wild and desolate sea-shore. That struck a chord in his memory, but he couldn't locate what he was thinking of.

They made their way among the boulders. It was easy to start with, but the nearer they came to the cliff the harder they had to search for ways up. As for Charles Madge, he could have gone any direction through the boulders or walked along the edge of the wood.

They stopped a stone's throw from the cliff proper after a particularly difficult piece of climbing. Johnny had had to give Daniel a leg up. Daniel had pulled Johnny up after him. The cliff loured over them. They couldn't see the trees on the cliff-top now, only the icy sky.

'Where now?' Johnny wondered. 'Up higher?'

'He could have followed the cliff round either way,' Daniel said, 'when he got out of the wood, left or right.'

'No,' Johnny said. 'He headed straight on up when he left the wood. I'll bet he did.'

'How did he?' Daniel said. 'This is a dead end.'

They scouted along the ledge of rock they were on, Daniel half-heartedly. But it was Daniel who shouted in a moment, 'We could just about manage it here.' Johnny came to see. Daniel had begun to scramble up the rock face. Suddenly he stopped and called out. 'Quick. Look up from where I'm standing,' he said. 'To the right.' He pointed to a place about half-way up the rest of the cliff.

'Look how old and grey the stone is where we are. But that patch is much lighter in colour, isn't it?'

There seemed to be a ledge there, partly protected by curtains of rock that prevented them seeing exactly what they were looking at.

'Let's go up and find out,' Johnny said. 'It's somewhere to head for.'

'If we can get over this bit I think we can make our way all the way up,' Daniel added. 'How's your head for heights?'

'Passable.' Johnny shuddered.

It was not easy, but five minutes later they were standing on a narrow shelf of rock that ran along the face of the cliff. The climb would have been easier for a man with longer legs and arms, but despite several near falls the boys had made it. They knelt and looked down the way they'd come. They could see from here that once long ago the massive boulders had been torn off the cliff which had finished much further out into the valley. They could trace the path of the canal away among the trees, but they could not see it.

Daniel began to shuffle along the ledge. The patch of stone that was much lighter than the rest was now lower than they were.

Daniel knelt down to look when they were directly above it. 'That's new rock, definitely,' he said. 'It hasn't weathered.'

'What do you mean?' Johnny said, holding back. The drop was considerable.

'I mean that if the sun had been shining on it and the rain pouring down on it for very long it would have gone grey like the rest before now. The colour our farm is, and your house and most of the houses in Summerfield for that matter.'

'You mean it's been uncovered recently?'

'That's right.'

'How recently?' Johnny's excitement grew.

'I can't tell that. I'm no expert,' Daniel said. 'But not long ago, I'd say. The stone around here weathers pretty fast. I remember Dad saying so once. Though how fast fast is for stone I don't know.'

'What might have uncovered it? Could Charles Madge have?'

'I shouldn't think so.' Daniel nodded doubtfully. 'He'd need dynamite to do a job like that, and why should he want to dynamite a bit of hillside out in the middle of nowhere anyway?' He lay down on his stomach and shoved his head over the ledge to see better. Johnny did the same. 'Perhaps he just came across it.'

'Came across it?' Johnny said. 'What would he have been doing here in the first place?' He gazed down too, trying to work out what it all meant. Then all of a sudden he called out: 'I can see what happened!' He lay down and hung his body over the edge as far as he dared. 'I'm sure I can. There's a crack that runs right down from below us, isn't there, through the centre of the lighter part?'

'Yes.'

'I can't see properly of course without going down, but the crack's quite deep I think. I've seen pictures like those after earthquakes.'

'No, not an earthquake,' Daniel said. 'But you've got the idea. Lightning! The hill's been struck by lightning. That's what's torn the hillside away here. Don't you remember – a couple of weeks ago there was the most tremendous thunderstorm one night. Hey, what's this?' Daniel rolled over on his side and began scrabbling in the earth he'd been lying on.

Johnny knelt up to see. 'A half-smoked cigarette,' he said. 'And I know who smoked it! Charles Madge. His cigarettes have a gold tip.' He leant over the edge again. 'Whatever's down there must be why Charles Madge brought his spade and pick axe.'

'Give me a hand,' Daniel said. 'We can get down there and see. Carefully though!' he added as Johnny prepared just to drop over the edge in his eagerness. 'That's a fifty foot drop if you miss the ledge. You'll break your neck.'

Soon they were standing in front of an opening in the rock that was just wide enough for one of them to slip through. It would be harder for Charles Madge, Johnny thought, which must be why he'd brought the pick-axe. There was evidence all around of the work he'd put in trying to widen the opening. The ledge they were standing on was littered with chippings of stone and the tell-tale cigarette ends. He must have spent hours here.

'Now we'll find the answers to our questions, perhaps,' Daniel said. 'Who's going in? You or me?'

IO

Without really knowing why it should be him, but it had to be, Johnny stooped and slid sideways into the crack. Going in was easier than he'd thought. He twisted and the rock let him through. The knack came to him straightaway.

He carefully straightened up inside. He could stand upright in the pitch-black darkness. There was a cave all right, but how high and long it was he had no idea. Not a scrap of light filtered through from outside, nor a sound.

So this was where Charles Madge had come. But why? What was in the cave that was so important?

He took a tentative step forward, hands outstretched to stop himself walking into anything. At his second step his wellingtons kicked something ahead of him across the cave floor. He tested with his toe. As best he could tell the ground was scattered with chippings of rock. Charles Madge had been using his pick-axe in here too.

Then there was a new sensation. Suddenly he was beginning to see. A pale light was slowly filling the cave. And there was something else that panicked him till he realised what it was. There was that feeling inside his head, the feeling he'd had out in the wood, an invading. He turned to make his getaway, but at the same time he saw and heard. He saw Kaa, the boy of his dreams and the children's stories, and he knew all of a sudden that the voice in his head was the voice of Kaa's thoughts. Kaa was at the far side of the cave, bent over his father who was dying from the injuries the wolf had inflicted. Kaa had somehow managed to drag his father up the rock-face to safety. All night he had lain here, but all the same he was dying now morning had come. This was what was in Kaa's thoughts, overwhelming everything else, even his own predicament. And now Kaa's father was whispering something to Kaa. Kaa put his ear down to his father's lips to catch the words. The words came to Johnny from Kaa's thoughts. 'The necklace – you must find it – without it you are lost and the people too. It must have dropped on the hill – among the trees. But it is not there – you will not find it there. Someone will help you. Tonight. Before the wolf comes.' 'Who?' Johnny felt Kaa say.

'A boy. Kaa, stay here. Stay here and wait, however long. Kaa – the necklace – you must have it. Without it you are no priest.'

Then there were no more words. Kaa's father was dead now and Johnny felt Kaa's grief well up and drown everything else. The grief lasted for Johnny didn't know how long of his own time, and Johnny cried too with the stranger boy.

At last Kaa stood up and looked in Johnny's direction. For a moment the sensation was too confusing, Kaa could see Johnny just as Johnny could see Kaa. Kaa flinched back and Johnny stepped forward to reassure him . . .

Then suddenly Johnny was no longer in the past. Daniel was standing in the darkened cave beside him. 'What was that light?' Daniel was saying. 'And who was that boy? He looked like an Eskimo. Johnny!'

When Johnny came to he found himself lying outside the cave gazing up into the pale wintry sky. He was shaking with cold from head to toe.

'You fainted,' Daniel said by way of explanation. 'What was going on? I shouted for ages, then I had to come in after you. I'd swear I saw a boy and someone lying on the floor, and then it was dark.'

'I'll tell you in a minute,' Johnny murmured, still gazing up into the sky. He wondered whether it was the sky now or the sky in Kaa's time, which Mrs Braithwaite had quite rightly said must have been during the Ice Age. Lying there he saw the precarious way Kaa had made his way down from the cliff-top.

After a moment, carefully avoiding looking back at the cave-entrance, he scrambled to his feet and crouched looking out across the wood. It was today's wood. He could see the path of the canal. 'It was a sort of vision,' he said to Daniel. 'That's what I saw. And you did too, the end of it.'

'A vision?' Daniel looked puzzled. 'You saw more than me then. It was gone in a flash. I just saw the boy who looked like an Eskimo and the figure lying on the floor, that's all.'

But Johnny's attention was caught by something at the bottom of the hillside. At first to his eye it was only a grey cloud-like shape among the scattered boulders. Then his eyes got it into focus. A wolf was glaring up at him and Daniel. There was no mistaking what it was. He'd seen a pack of them once at the zoo. But here at Yonderley? How did it come to be here? Had it escaped from the zoo?

He stepped back towards the cave-mouth in panic as the wolf bared its teeth and began to run. It leaped where Johnny and Daniel had laboriously climbed. Then suddenly, as abruptly as it had appeared, it faded away. Yet it had been there, solid and real as Johnny and Daniel themselves for a moment, as real as the wintry wood that surrounded them . . .

—— *11* ——

'Where've you been?' Dad grumbled, pointing to his watch. 'I've been waiting for ages. It's sweltering in this heat.' He looked more closely at the pair panting by the open window of the car. 'Are you all right? Has something happened?'

'No, Dad, nothing, honestly,' Johnny said, trying to control his hectic breathing. He felt numb after what had happened but he didn't want to show it. Both he and Daniel were cold too, frozen to the bone, however hot Dad found it. 'Come on, Daniel. Let's get in.' He pushed Daniel round the other side of the car, then clambered in the back seat after him.

Dad started the car. He'd already turned it round to point in the right direction. 'What have you two found to do, then?' he asked.

'The canal's just along the road, Dad,' Johnny said, his heart in his mouth at having to say this. 'We went exploring again.'

'The canal – ' Dad said. He turned round to have a closer look at the boys, then sighed. 'That explains the dirt then. At your age you'd think you'd manage to keep cleaner.' He put the car into gear and moved off the verge into the lane. 'You said earlier this week there was something odd over here, didn't you?'

'Yes, Dad,' Johnny said, his heart in his mouth again.

'All the trees losing their leaves, wasn't it, or something unseasonal like that? What about the thing you thought was moving in the woods?'

'Nothing, Dad.'

'I thought not!' Dad said. 'You would hardly have gone back if there was, would you?'

Johnny managed a short laugh. How close Dad was to the truth, but Johnny dared not risk telling him it now he knew he wasn't involved in all this by chance. 'There will be someone to help you – a boy,' Kaa's father had said. Who else could that boy be but Johnny? If Johnny was the link between past and present he couldn't risk his father saying, 'You mustn't go over to Yonderley any more,' even if it meant keeping things from Dad or even deceiving him.

But Dad still stayed close to the track. 'Heard anything more about those stories at school, have you?' he said. 'You wrote one of them, didn't you, Daniel?'

'Yes, I did,' Daniel said.

'Mrs Braithwaite hasn't risked any more stories!' Johnny said.

'I bet not!' Dad laughed. 'I wouldn't either if I were her!'

They had passed in and out of Yonderley. Soon they were on the top of Denver. At the start of the descent Dad stopped the car to look at the view. 'Not often I come up here,' he said. The two boys shivered while he admired the hills, but luckily when he started off down the lane he'd forgotten all about the canal.

After they'd dropped off Daniel Johnny began to think about what had happened in the cave. How was he to help Kaa? Kaa's father had said that Kaa himself wouldn't find the necklace. But if Johnny was meant to find it, where was he to look? Kaa's father had said it wasn't where it had been lost. That was confusing. And if he found it, how was he to give it back? How could he give it to a sort of ghost?

'Your Uncle Charles is in,' Dad remarked, cutting into Johnny's thoughts.

Johnny looked up quickly and saw they were home and that the Land Rover was there too. He'd forgotten about Madge and seeing him by the canal bridge and all the subsequent things they'd found out. Something more important had intervened. But Johnny had to think about him now. Why hadn't Madge told him last night that he'd already been over to the canal as he so obviously had? And what had he been digging for in the cave?

'Out you get,' Dad said. 'I expect tea's waiting. I'm more than ready for it.'

Had Madge seen Kaa too? Johnny asked himself. He must have. That would explain why he was being so secretive with Johnny's parents, yet it didn't explain how he had found the cave in the first place. And it didn't explain either why Madge had confided nothing in Johnny last night when he'd had the chance. But then perhaps he hadn't bargained on Johnny going over and seeing Kaa – it wasn't the kind of secret you told to anyone who wasn't already completely in the know, not until you knew you could trust them. Thinking like this left Johnny in an agony of doubt about his cousin. Perhaps Madge had been right to be secretive. Perhaps Johnny in the same position would have acted in the same way.

'Just in time,' Mum said as he and Dad came in through the back door. 'You must have smelt it cooking.'

'The job took longer than I expected,' Dad explained. 'What a day though – the temperature must be in the nineties.' He didn't mention the two boys had made him late.

'Your friend better now?' Mum asked. She was busy turning gas-rings off and producing hot plates for the food.

'Up and about,' Dad said. 'He'll be back at work soon now. Charles round here or next door?'

'Here,' Charles Madge's voice rang out from the hall. He stood by Johnny who was keeping his dirty trousers out of Mum's sight. Johnny started, not having heard him arrive.

'Did you have an interesting day at school?' Charles Madge asked Johnny. He probably meant had there been any more strange stories about Kaa, but Johnny was too confused to know.

'Okay,' he said. He hadn't thought to tell Dad not to say anything about the canal in front of Charles Madge, but there was no way he could have done so. The next moment Charles Madge knew where Johnny had been.

'Have you been helping Dad?' Mum said.

Dad gave Johnny no chance to answer.

'Oh there was no need for that. I could manage on my own,' Dad said. 'We picked Daniel up on the way and he and Johnny went exploring the canal again.'

'The canal?' Mum said. 'Again?'

'Yes, it seems to have some fascination for them. We should go some day for a picnic. I don't think we've ever taken Johnny. I seem to remember it was quite interesting. In fact I've got a book somewhere about the canal. A very old one.'

Johnny's back was to Madge so he couldn't see how he'd taken this, but his cousin said, 'Perhaps I'll be able to come along with you. It's about time I got to know some of these back lanes. I've never been over Yonderley way.'

'Why yes, of course you can,' Mum said. 'You've no need to ask.'

The lie was so coolly spoken Johnny could have congratulated him. But then of course Madge didn't know he'd been seen. 'Excuse me, I'll just wash my hands,' Johnny said, moving quickly from the kitchen into the hall past Madge. 'I won't be a minute.'

He scuttled upstairs, half-expecting to be followed. Madge was sure to want to talk to him again now. When he did, how should he act? Let him know he'd been seen? So much had been explained and muddled up again this afternoon. Even if Johnny knew now he had to help Kaa, he hadn't the faintest idea how to go about it and perhaps Madge did. Perhaps Madge already knew where the necklace was. That decided Johnny. He had to talk to him as soon as possible.

He slipped a jumper on before coming down. It might be warm outside in the sun, but in the house he felt chilled to the bone as if he was still at the canal in the middle of the winter wood.

The three grown-ups were sitting at table. The jumper was a mistake. Mum took one look. 'What are you doing wearing that?' she said.

'I felt cold, that's all,' Johnny said.

'Wish I did!' Dad laughed. 'It's not been warmer this summer to my mind.'

Mum put a hand on Johnny's, then quickly felt his cheek. 'You're right. You're freezing!' she said.

'Freezing?' Dad looked puzzled. 'How can he be?' He laid his hand on Johnny's too.

'You're not sickening for something, are you?' Mum asked. 'You look all right in yourself. Are you?'

'Yes, perfectly,' Johnny said, mad with himself. He had given away that he'd been up to something odd, and also told Charles Madge he'd been in the coldest part of the wood. His cousin gave him a long questioning stare. The blood ran into Johnny's cheeks. He was not managing this very well.

'The canal runs out through a valley and some woods, doesn't it?' Charles Madge said, speaking for the first time since Johnny's appearance. 'I've been looking at the map. Woods do stay cool this time of the year. They always seem to be a couple of days behind with their weather. You'll warm up soon enough, Johnny.'

'I daresay he will, Charles,' Dad said.

Rescued, Johnny got on with his meal. True enough, with the sweater on he began to warm up soon. But then, Madge would know – he'd just been through the same experience. The attention had passed away completely from Johnny by now. Madge was talking about surfing in Australia, and Mum was talking about a holiday she'd had in North Wales when she was a girl. Madge was certainly a very cool customer, Johnny thought. He couldn't make him out. What was he up to? Johnny knew why he was being mysterious himself, but why was Madge? Another question kept taxing him, and it had mystified Daniel too – how had Madge found the cave in the first place? By chance, or design? It could only be by chance. But what a chance to have found that cave and the person he was staying with to have found it too!

'Johnny!' Mum was saying in exasperation. 'We're trying to talk to you!'

'What?' Johnny looked up, startled out of his thoughts.

'We were saying you'll be on holiday from Saturday,' Mum said. 'Perhaps you and Uncle Charles would like to go out together. It's all very well him spending his days in the library reading up the history of the district, but it's about time he had a look at the places he's going to write about.'

'Oh, I'll have plenty of time for that,' Charles Madge said quickly. Johnny knew immediately why he was squashing Mum's idea – he wanted people to think he was at the library while he had as much freedom as he wanted to be over at Yonderley. Then he added, equally quickly, 'Anyway, Johnny's got six or seven weeks off. When I've my papers in order he and I and his friend Daniel can explore the countryside all we want.'

'You've met Daniel?' Mum said.

'Not yet,' Madge said. 'I'm looking forward to having the pleasure.'

The meal came and went. Johnny didn't taste a thing. he couldn't even have named what he'd eaten. Sometime during the pudding he removed his sweater – no one noticed. 'Enjoy your meal?' Mum said. 'Yes, Mum,' he replied, but how could he think of food when there was this strange thing that had come into his life? He thought of Kaa bent over his dying father and even though it had happened hundreds and thousands of years ago a lump came into his throat. It was all he could do to stop himself from crying.

A little later after the dishes had been cleared Johnny found he was sitting alone with Madge. Johnny stiffened. Now they had to talk.

Madge was clearly aware of this too. He leant forward and spoke softly up the length of the table.

'You went over there again, then.'

Johnny nodded. He was full of anticipation as to what Charles Madge would say.

'Brave of you,' Madge said. 'I wouldn't be so brave, not after what you told me.'

Johnny looked away from his cousin – was he going to keep up the pretence with him? But why? Didn't he trust him?

'You want to be careful,' Madge went on. 'If all those things you told me about the canal are connected as you thought – ' as you made me think, Johnny thought, ' – there might be danger there, considerable danger. These happenings are best not meddled with. Believe me, I know.' He came round the table and sat in the chair next to Johnny at the same time glancing at the door where Mum and Dad might appear any moment. 'Keep well away – that's my advice. I've thought about this. I was hasty last night, talking as I did.'

Johnny looked him straight in the face for the first time since he'd lied. Had his last words been meant as a kindly warning or an underhand threat? It wasn't easy to tell from Madge's friendly tone of voice. Why did Madge want to keep the wood and the cave to himself? It wasn't after all a question of trust.

Then he added innocently, a sort of by-the-way, 'And when you were down there, was there anything that might tie in with what you already thought?'

'But you've been down there yourself,' Johnny blurted out. He couldn't help it. 'You should know.' He couldn't keep it in.

'Me? Don't —'

'Daniel and I saw you!' Johnny said.

'Saw me?' For a moment Charles Madge was going to protest that Johnny and Daniel were most assuredly mistaken, but then he saw it was no use. He sighed and then said, most sincerely, 'I'm sorry to have deceived you. Really I am. But what did you see? How far did you go? There was a little cottage near the canal tunnel entrance. It got too cold there for me. I had to turn back. What about – ?' Then an expression of disappointment passed across Madge's face. Johnny swivelled round to follow his gaze.

'Coffee for you, Charles,' Mum said. 'What about you, Johnny?'

'No thanks, Mum,' Johnny said. He got up. 'I think I'll go upstairs. I've one or two things to do.'

He lingered outside the door a moment. He heard Madge say, 'A bright lad you've got there,' soft-soaping Mum, and he remembered how he hadn't altogether trusted Madge the first time he'd met him - now he had real solid reason not to. It was just one lie after another.

Madge laughed at something Mum said, and Johnny heard for the first time just how false that laugh was.

—12—

Charles Madge typed every night from about nine. Johnny could always hear him from his bedroom at the back of the house, but that night he could hear it extra-clearly. Probably it was because he was especially aware of his cousin. Then suddenly Johnny was drifting off to sleep, the sounds of the typewriter keys receding, without even having had time to think of Kaa and what he could do for him.

Kaa.

In his dream Johnny was back with Kaa.

Thick grey clouds hung over the hill and the little valley.

On all fours Kaa crept along the valley rim, the cave left behind him. *My father is dead, the necklace is lost, the people will die. I must find the necklace*. This message echoed through his brain.

Kaa tried not to think of the cave where his father now lay dead, or of the spirit he'd seen in it, or of the wolf that would come for him this night.

His eyes missed nothing as he crept along. He saw signs on the ground of every step he and his father had taken. He saw where he'd missed his footing and recovered it. He saw where his father had stood a moment to sniff out the lie of the land. And it wasn't only his eyes that were aware – every rustle from the wood told him something, every breath of breeze that reached his nose.

Kaa reached the spot where he had come out of the woods the

night before and found the valley below his feet. He stopped and crouched there thinking. There had been no sign of the necklace. It would be in the wood then. Kaa looked up at the sky. It was dark for midday. What had his father said?

'It must have dropped on the hill – among the trees – but it is not there, you will not find it – there will be someone to help you. A boy. Stay and wait, however long.'

Kaa stood up. He had take a decision. His father had known the future so he must do what his father said. He would go back to the cave and stay and wait. It would be wrong of him to put his own fear before the future of the people.

He turned back the way he had come. He would bury his father before nightfall and then await what came.

In the morning it was last day of school, a day without work except for handing in books and moving to new classrooms for the coming September. Usually Johnny enjoyed last days, like anyone else, but that Friday passed in a haze. His mind was entirely taken up with Kaa and Madge and Yonderley. He had to find the necklace for Kaa – that was obvious. And it had to be him to give it to Kaa – that seemed obvious too. But the task of searching the whole of the top of the hill seemed an impossibility, and if Kaa was only a sort of vision how could he hand a necklace to that?

After school as he approached the house from the bus stop he saw that as usual Charles Madge's Land Rover had gone and then, as he raced down by the side of the house, he saw something else that made him pull up short. There was a line of brown running through the woods along the skyline on the top of Denver. Or was he just imagining it? He stared until his eyes hurt.

Inside, speaking as casually as he could considering it was so important, he asked Mum if she could see it too.

'Yes, I think you're right,' she said. 'I wonder what it can be. It almost looks as if it's been burnt.'

'Going to Daniel's,' he shouted as he left. He was sure, the more he looked, that the brown patch was there.

Then he noticed an odd thing as he got his bike out of the potting-shed. Long pieces of grass, quite fresh, were entangled in the spokes of the back wheel, and however much he racked his brain he couldn't remember having had the bike out for several days. Sunday, five days ago, had been the last time. For a moment he puzzled over it – it looked almost as if someone had borrowed the bike – then he gave up and wheeled the bike into the lane.

'Madge isn't in,' he said to Daniel as he dismounted at the farm gate. 'Are we going up the hill, then?' The mystery of the grass in his wheels had driven the brown line on the top of Denver out of his mind.

'We've got to find this necklace, haven't we?' Daniel said. 'You've talked about nothing else all day. I wish Dad was in. He's always out when you want him most. He was too busy last night to talk. The sheep up in the top field were really restless. He thought there might be a fox or dog hanging about, but it wasn't there. Anyway, come over this side of the gate!'

Johnny climbed over and joined him in the shade of the wall. 'I'm sure your cousin has the key to it all,' Daniel went on. 'He seems to know exactly what he's doing. It's a pity you couldn't have had it out with him last night. Maybe he knows where the necklace is.'

'If he does, why should he tell me?' Johnny said. 'He's told me nothing so far except lies.'

'He put you on the trail,' Daniel said. 'He suggested to you there might be a connection between everything. We might not have gone over to Yonderley again if he hadn't. Remember that.'

Johnny sighed. 'Then he warned me off. I think he regretted having put the idea into my mind. I don't trust him.'

'He may still be genuine,' Daniel said. 'Just because someone's keeping quiet about something doesn't mean they're bad. You're keeping quiet about it too, aren't you? Now how are we going to find this necklace? We're wasting time here. Are we going to search the woods? And I still think you're being hasty about your cousin.'

'Kaa already searched them in my dream,' Johnny said.

'No further than the head of the valley,' Daniel reminded him. 'Or at least you said so at school when you told me about your dream. That leaves the whole hill to search.' He laughed. 'That's plenty to be going on with.'

'It would be buried feet deep in earth by now. I asked Mr Waldron at school about that without telling him why I wanted to know,' Johnny said. 'And we can't dig up the hill. It'll be like looking for a needle in a haystack.'

'But we can't wait for it to come to us,' Daniel replied. 'That's why I wish you'd talk to your Australian cousin again, however you feel. It's hopeless as it stands. He must know something more than us. He got there first.'

'He only arrived the night after the first time we went to Yonderley,' Johnny pointed out. He stood up and stretched. 'All right. Maybe we ought to give the hill a try,' he said. 'We can't hope to work out the path Kaa and his father took, but we can wander at random. If lightning opened the cave and both Madge and I chanced on it, perhaps there's a chance we might stumble on the necklace too.'

'You're right,' Daniel said. 'Luck's been on your side so far.'

Then Johnny remembered at last. 'And there's another thing. The trees at the very top of the hill were darkening. At least it seemed so from our house. Mum thought so too.'

'On the top of Denver?' Daniel looked very serious. 'That means it's coming towards our farm. Come on,' he said, jumping up immediately. 'You should have said so at once. We've got to go and check. Then, if you're right Dad's got to know at once. Why didn't you tell me straightaway?'

High on Denver that afternoon there was no breeze and not a cloud in the sky. It was even hotter, if that were possible, than yesterday. Stripped to their waists the two boys toiled upwards, one thought only in their minds now – to see if the desolation that had started at the cave was moving as fast over Denver towards the farm as it seemed to be. They didn't talk as they rode the track upwards. Johnny felt guilty he hadn't seen how important this was to the Butlers' farm. Daniel was just plain anxious. They weren't searching for the necklace. They were in too much hurry – there was something else more important than that. Or at least it seemed so.

They breasted the rise and were onto Denver's flat top. At the gate into the wood they left their bikes – remembering their last ride over and how neglected the track was – and continued on foot. They didn't have to go far, a few hundred yards, before they saw their first evidence that Johnny had been right. On some trees, though not all, leaves were yellowing. The air grew cooler too – they had to pull their shirts back on. Another hundred yards, on the downward slope before the cave valley rim, it was as bad as they'd seen in the valley itself yesterday.

'No, needn't go any further,' Daniel said, breaking the silence. 'We might as well go back and tell Dad. This is spreading like wild-fire.'

'Why is it spreading so much faster this way though?' Johnny said.

'I don't know and at this moment I don't care. At this rate the farm will be engulfed in days,' Daniel said. 'Unless there's some way of stopping it.'

'Like what?' Johnny said.

'If only I knew!' Daniel replied despairingly. That made Johnny think. Maybe the way to stop it was through Kaa. If they found the necklace and gave it back to him, then would the cold . . . It was a stray thought. He didn't complete it.

Then he heard a sound. He touched Daniel's arm to warn him.

It was very silent in this part of the wood, just as it had been among the trees in the valley yesterday. Johnny held his breath.

'I hope it's not your Kaa friend again,' Daniel said loudly. 'We haven't time for that.'

'Sshh! Listen!' Johnny put his fingers to his lips. 'It wasn't Kaa.' He heard the noise again. There was movement, quite definitely, among the autumn trees down towards the valley rim.

Daniel heard it too. He paled. 'The wolf?' he said anxiously.

They heard the movement more clearly now. It was coming

towards them. It was a careful, heavy step.

'A person,' Johnny whispered. 'I'm sure it is.'

They were both prepared to run for it though.

A man came out from a hollow among the trees and looked around as he reached the track. His eyes till then had been glued to the ground.

It was Charles Madge.

He saw them.

'Johnny! How nice to see you!' he called and hastened towards them.

'So this is your friend Daniel?' he said. 'Johnny's told me a lot about you.'

Charles Madge was dressed up warm in a winter anorak with a fur-lined hood. He had leather mittens on his hands and was balancing one of his gold-tipped cigarettes between the thick fingers and making a cloud of steam and smoke in the cold air.

'Where's your Land Rover?' Johnny asked. He felt tongue-tied knowing what he'd been saying about Madge to Daniel today, and so he just blurted out the first thing that came into his head.

'Down where you saw it yesterday,' Madge said. He seated himself on a fallen tree-trunk and looked up at the two boys. 'This track's a bit rough even for a Land Rover with four-wheel drive. I'm sorry about not telling you yesterday that I'd been down to the canal as well as you,' he said. 'I'm a journalist. It's my natural instinct to keep quiet about anything out of the ordinary, at least until it's in the papers with my signature on the article.'

'In the paper?' Johnny said.

'Not in this case, of course,' Madge said quickly. 'First of all I'm out of newspapers now, as you know. And secondly I can't see anyone being interested in this. No, as I say, it was just my instinct not to say anything to you. That's my apology anyway. I hope you accept it.'

'Why yes,' Johnny said quickly. He was trying to work out what no one would be interested in – the winter wood, or Kaa. But Madge hadn't mentioned Kaa or anything to do with him, except two nights ago in connection with the dream. As for Johnny, he thought that people would be interested, and in both.

Madge said nothing more, but just sat there gazing around at the stripped branches bathed in heatless wintry sunlight. Daniel glanced at Johnny, trying to convey that he ought to try to find out more. But Johnny was puzzled – why didn't Madge ever mention Kaa? Kaa was what this was all about. Why was he still pretending to have only gone to Yonderley for the first time yesterday? His suspicions of the man deepened further.

'What are you doing up here?' Daniel asked after a final look at Johnny.

'Doing up here?' Madge replied. He gave Daniel a smile that suddenly seemed to Johnny as false as could be. It looked like so many of those smiles that he had given Mum and Dad and himself.

'I mean, it's not a very nice place for a walk,' Daniel went on.

'Nor for you.'

'It's getting near my father's land.'

'You mean this disease, or whatever it is, is spreading?'

Johnny knew then, if he hadn't known it before, that all he would get from Madge was lies. Madge had to know it was spreading. Daniel had spotted this too – he raised his eyebrows at Johnny.

'I was having a look round, seeing its limits,' Madge replied in answer to Daniel's question about why he was here in the first place. 'I don't know what's causing these trees to wither – ' he shivered and smiled, '– and this cold, but it would be interesting to find out.'

He had been looking on the ground before he reached the track. Had he been looking for the same thing that he wanted himself? Johnny suddenly thought. Was he after the necklace?

Madge got up and stretched. 'You two must be freezing,' he said. 'You don't want to be icy to the touch when you get home for tea, do you, Johnny?' He wrapped his coat more tightly around him, then added: 'I would keep away if I were you. Something funny's going on here. You don't know what might happen to you yourself. A disease. That's what it probably is.'

'A disease?' Johnny said innocently. That had been his first idea and Daniel's, but they'd soon changed their minds – the change in the weather and the cold seemed to have made the difference.

'An infection of some kind perhaps,' Madge added. 'I heard of something similar in Australia once. Played havoc for a while, then all of a sudden died out. Now off you go – and remember: keep away. Let me deal with this.'

The boys turned to go, and Madge too. Then he called after them, 'No more of your strange feelings down the canal yesterday, Johnny? Can't say I felt a thing.'

'No nothing,' Johnny called. 'It must have just been my imagination. It's pretty creepy down there.'

'Quite so,' Madge said. Johnny sensed disappointment on his face. 'And your dreams?'

'Stopped,' Johnny said. 'See you later.'

When the boys were out of sight they broke into a run. A hundred yards out of the wood they threw themselves down panting on the grass.

'You were really right not to trust him,' Daniel gasped. 'What a liar! All that stuff about something similar happening in Australia – he made that up on the spot! What he really wants is for us not to go down there. He's trying to frighten us off. He couldn't care less if we caught pneumonia or not!'

'Each time he's talked to me he's wanted to find out as much of what I know as he can without telling me anything,' Johnny said. 'Is he searching for the necklace like us? That means he's seen Kaa. And if he hasn't seen Kaa, why would he want the necklace? And how could he have known about it before I told him?'

Daniel sat up. 'On our bikes,' he said. 'Dad next. I'm afraid we've got to forget Kaa and the necklace and your cousin for now. What happens if it does reach the farm?' He pointed back to the wood. 'Who knows, it might reach here tomorrow at its present rate.'

But Mr Butler was not at the farm. 'If you've just come down the hill I don't know how you missed him.' Daniel's mother looked puzzled. 'I saw him go up the track myself. Straight in from town, and then up Denver. He was in such a hurry he left one of the gates open.'

There seemed nothing to do except go back the way they'd come. They abandoned their bikes half-way up, tired of opening gates and fighting against the slope, and they were right back in the last field without having seen him. Then Johnny spotted a windscreen reflecting light several wide fields away towards Summerfield.

'That's strange,' Daniel said. 'He's taken it into the field that's above the canal cutting on this side of the hill. What is Dad up to? We haven't used that particular field for anything for years.'

They ran down the hillside, collected their bikes and cycled straight across the grass through a herd of bullocks to the gate into the next field. Two fields away they reached the Land Rover, though when they got there there was still no sign of Mr Butler.

'Let's leave our bikes again,' Daniel said. 'I think Dad must have gone down into the canal cutting, though I can't think why. If I'm wrong he'll see our bikes when he gets back and know we're searching for him.'

'Could it be something to do with why we've come looking for him?' Johnny said. He was suddenly full of foreboding.

'Who knows?' Daniel said. 'Let's try and find out.'

The cutting this side of the hill was more gently sided and shallow than the valley over near Yonderley. The two boys found an easy way down a channel where water ran off the field above during torrentially rainy weather.

Half-way down they came to a rock that jutted out and Daniel shouted. His voice echoed back lazily. At last there came an answering shout from among the trees below.

'There was a touch of brown about some of the treetops,' Mr Butler said, wiping sweat off his brow though it was much colder in the bottom than on the hill above. 'If it happened that side of the hill, it could happen this. I came over to investigate. A good job I did. It's obviously hitting at random all over the hill now.' He kicked at the undergrowth that had gone the same way as the wood on the opposite side of the hill. It was in the first autumnal stage. 'This is practically on my land now and I've got to do something about it. First I'll take some of this back with me for samples, then I'll ring the Ministry of Agriculture people – if they haven't gone home already.'

Johnny nudged Daniel.

'What?' Daniel whispered.

'Let's leave Kaa and the cave and the wolf out of what we say.' At the mention of the Ministry of Agriculture Johnny had had an awful vision of dozens of men poking about the cave and getting in the way of his finding the necklace. And as much as he trusted Mr Butler he couldn't quite see him taking the same attitude to Kaa as he and Daniel were. Wouldn't Kaa in a roundabout way be Mr Butler's enemy?

'I think you're right,' Daniel whispered back.

Mr Butler sighed. He was too full of his own thoughts to have noticed tham talking. 'I'll feel such a fool,' he said. 'What shall I tell them? July frosts? They'll make a laughing-stock out of me. Lucky I know one of them quite well. Even so he'll think I'm trying to play some particularly silly practical joke.'

He began moving back up the bank and the boys followed him.

Now it was getting public and whatever Charles Madge had said about it being of no interest to newspapers, Johnny knew differently. As the news spread, which it was sure to now, local people were going to flock to see what was happening.

Mr Butler called back. 'At this rate every tree on the hill's going to be dead within a month and there's not going to be a blade of grass for the sheep and cattle to eat. My farm's going to be a desert.'

'A desert,' Daniel said. 'That's just how Lisa's story described the hills in Kaa's time.'

13

Johnny was having breakfast on his own next morning when he heard Mum call Dad into the back room. He didn't take any notice till he realised they were watching someting interesting outside.

He left his breakfast unfinished and joined them. Mum was pointing to something low on Denver and Dad was saying he couldn't quite see, but Johnny knew what must be going on. Partly hidden from view by a huge tree on the other side of the lane below their house there were several vehicles parked near the top of the invisible canal embankment. The Ministry of Agriculture men had come then. Johnny took a long look, then went straight back to gobble down his meal.

'Goodbye,' he called a little later from the back room door. 'I'm going down Daniel's.'

'All right, but don't be too late for dinner,' Mum said. 'We're all going out after to Aunt Harriet's. Uncle Charles too.'

'Really?' Johnny said. His face fell at the idea of having to go out, but maybe he would be able to wriggle out of it. He left that battle to later though.

'Any idea what's going on over there?' Dad said, calling Johnny back. 'Your friend's farm seems a hive of activity this morning.'

'It's that sort of disease Daniel and I saw over at Yonderley,' Johnny explained. 'It's spread over here.' He used the word 'disease' purposely – it was less extraordinary than 'change in the weather.'

'*That*!' Dad said. 'I remember you told me about it the day Charles arrived, and a couple of days ago – when I took you over to Yonderley. How amazing. I felt sure you were exaggerating.'

'So did Mr Butler at first,' Johnny said.

'A *plant* disease?' Mum asked. 'It can't hurt people, can it?'

'Oh no,' Johnny said. 'Mr Butler found it in the canal bottom yesterday and he let both Daniel and me go down with him.'

'That's all right then.' Mum sounded relieved.

'So Johnny was right then,' Dad said. 'He does seem to be turning up some odd things recently. There were those dreams and the stories at school. Remember? Now this plant disease – '

Johnny didn't stop for a discussion. Again Dad was unwittingly getting very close to the mark for someone who didn't believe in anything ghostly! Only the worry that Dad might keep him off Denver stopped him from telling Dad about everything, including Madge.

After the swiftest descent ever down the hill, he left his bike hidden in the hedge at the bottom of the lane, then made his way on foot over and up the hill towards the vehicles. Not many minutes later he was there. Daniel was sitting on the engine of his Dad's Land Rover, chewing a long piece of grass and looking rather bored and left out of it. There were three vehicles; Mr Butler's Land Rover, another Land Rover and a shooting-brake. Four men including Mr Butler were standing by them. They were in deep conversation except for one who was kneeling down in the grass, carefully taking samples of the grass which he was putting with roots and soil into plastic bags. Daniel, obviously, was being ignored.

He greeted Johnny rapturously. 'I never thought you'd come,' he said. 'You can see here from your house, can't you? I was hoping you would.'

Johnny pointed at the man taking samples. To judge by the number of filled polythene bags beside him it looked as if he'd nearly finished his job. 'It's all right here, isn't it?' he said. They were about thirty yards from the edge of the field and everything here looked normal. 'What are they doing?'

'They had a quick look over the bank, then came straight back,' Daniel said. 'They're collecting samples of earth and plants here, then going down the canal to get others to compare. But they're taking so long over it.'

'And what do they think?' Johnny said quickly.

'They're totally mystified. They haven't the faintest idea what's wrong,' Daniel said. 'None of them have seen anything like it before. See that man with glasses and rather bald on top? He's the friend Dad mentioned yesterday. They were at agricultural college together. He's an expert on foreign plants and plant diseases that get carried into England, but he's seen nothing like it either. If anyone can find out what it is, he's the one to do it, Dad says.'

The group of men began moving towards the edge of the field. The first of them disappeared over the edge of the cutting. They'd fallen silent now.

'The same's happening over here,' Daniel continued, 'as on the other side of the hill. Everything's beginning to die now and it had hardly started yesterday. It's almost like it must have been between the first and second times we went to Yonderley. It's cold, too, and the sun's watery if you look up at the sky from there. Though I haven't heard any of them mention it. They just can't have noticed it yet.'

'What if it all dies like over at Yonderley?' Johnny said. 'What's your Dad going to do?'

'He's worried to death,' Daniel said. 'He thinks the whole farm's going to be ruined.'

Johnny thought briefly of Kaa. Somehow Kaa was the cause of all this – but he couldn't tell Mr Butler or the experts that, on the one hand for Kaa's sake, on the other because they'd never believe him.

'Shall we follow them?' he asked Daniel.

'Yes!' Daniel jumped down off the Land Rover bonnet.

They walked across in the hot sun to the edge of the field, bracing themselves for the cool air to come. The men were out of sight below on the bank, though their voices drifted back up disjointedly. Johnny and Daniel began to go down. In a moment they spotted the others gathered round a bush whose leaves were brown and autumnal. One of the men shook it and a leaf drifted to the ground. 'Autumn,' one of them said in the middle of his sentence.

Involuntarily Johnny shivered. He looked up to the sky. As Daniel had said it was quite overcast here. What if it didn't stop spreading? What if it went on and on?

They went down past the men, then came round below. None of them took any notice of the boys. They were far too interested in what they were examining.

'There seems nothing wrong with it,' one of the men was saying, the bald-headed one Daniel had pointed out. 'No marks, no evidence of insects or larvae, or of any kind of infection.'

'But it's dying off,' another protested. 'Nothing could be clearer than that.'

'It looks to me as if it's closing down for winter,' the bald-headed man said. 'What this bush would naturally do in September or October when the frosts came.'

The man who had been taking samples gave a short bark of a laugh. 'I might remind you it's July. That's ridiculous!'

'Ridiculous it might be,' the bald-headed man said, 'but that's the way it seems. My bet is when we get some of this cut up and under a microscope we'll see that it's as I've said.'

'You make it sound like the Ice Age has come back,' the argumentative man went on. 'But why just here? Explain that. Why isn't the whole of England like this?'

'My Dad's friend thinks the same as us,' Daniel whispered, but something the last man had said had set off a chain of thoughts in Johnny's mind. The wintry hill – Kaa – the wolf – everything stemmed from the opening of the cave and the reason Kaa or his ghost still lingered there The necklace might be the key then not just to Kaa's problems, but to Mr Butler's too.

'The Ice Age,' Johnny said. 'Think! Kaa comes from then. Mrs Braithwaite said Lisa's story sounded like it was set then, and you said something similar yesterday.'

'Yes,' Daniel said. 'But . . .'

'It fits in with an idea I had after we met Madge yesterday!' Johnny was feeling more and more that he was right. 'I think the whole hill is going back to what it was like when Kaa was alive. The reason it's going back is Kaa, and all the tests those experts are going to make aren't going to tell them that. Giving the necklace back to to Kaa will stop the winter weather spreading, nothing else.'

'You mean that until we settle with Kaa this will go on?' Daniel said doubtfully.

'Yes!'

'If you're right we've got to tell Dad then. If you're right he's wasting his time with the Ministry of Agriculture.' He wrinkled up his forehead. 'It's an incredible idea.'

'It fits everything we know, doesn't it?' Johnny said. 'And you heard what your Dad's friend said. He said it wasn't a disease. He said it was what naturally happens in October or November, but it's happening in July. What causes that? *Cold*, not disease. What's caused the cold? Kaa and the opening of the cave! It's simple!'

'Hey you lads!' One of the men in the group had noticed them and was calling. 'Don't wander off too far. We don't know what this is all about yet.'

Daniel pulled Johnny's arm. 'Let's go and talk about it.'

The two lads went much lower down the bank until the men were out of sight. They were down by the canal itself.

'Now, come on,' Daniel said. 'Let's pool what we know. I've got to get it straight before you or I tell Dad. What you said sounded right to me, but it's got to sound right to Dad too. Tell me again. If you're right we need him to help us find the necklace.'

But Johnny wasn't listening. There, almost at his feet, was a patch of mud. That in itself was unusual after several days now of intense heat. But what struck Johnny more was a firm, deep paw mark in the middle of it. It was large, like a big dog's, but larger still and extremely clearly outlined. A heavy animal had made it.

'Look,' he said. 'What's that?'

'What – ' Daniel saw it too. He knelt down immediately. Then he jumped up and looked hastily around.'

'It looks fresh,' he said. 'How fresh I wonder.' He looked around again, very carefully.

'What is it?' Then suddenly Johnny thought he knew. 'Is it the – '

'Wolf!' Daniel finished his sentence. 'That wolf we saw? I'd bet my last penny on it.'

'It was only a misty sort of thing when we saw it though,' Johnny said. 'Now if it can leave marks it must have become solid. All that's happened in forty-eight hours. I wonder if this was your ghost at the farm? And there was another night I saw the sheep moving strangely in the field above here – when was it? Yes, Wednesday night when Charles Madge put all those ideas in my head. And your Dad had to come up here the night after.'

'Kaa must be the key to all this,' Daniel said. 'He's got to be. The wolf – Kaa – the cold – they're part of the same thing.'

They froze. Something had rustled the bushes behind them.

Johnny's heart pounded. He slowly swung in the direction the sound had come from. 'The wolf!' He wanted to call out, but his mouth was too dry to speak. Then he saw a coat. He laughed out loud to Daniel with relief. It was only one of the men.

But it wasn't one of the men. It was Charles Madge who stepped from behind the bushes.

He spoke very low. 'I saw them from the house,' he said. 'What are they? Agricultural experts?'

In shock at this sudden apparition Johnny nodded.

'You haven't told them about over there?' Charles Madge went on. 'About Yonderley?'

More collected now, Johnny looked across at Daniel wondering whether to tell him yes or no, but then he also wondered what exactly Madge meant by Yonderley.

'They know about the winter weather over there,' Johnny said cautiously. 'Or at least Daniel's father does – he's probably told them.'

'Nothing else?' Madge said.

'What else might there be?' Johnny asked, taking a deep breath.

Madge gave Johnny a straight searching look, then he looked at Daniel too. He knew immediately they knew more than he'd thought.

'Your dreams – the stories – the thing you thought was coming through the woods – ' He searched their faces to see if there was more he should admit to.

'And the cave and the boy who was trapped in it,' Johnny said.

'You found the cave then,' Madge said. 'I did too – yesterday, after I left you. You worked out your dreams were something to do with it. That's very good. I thought you were sensitive to these psychic events. That's why I wanted you to keep away since you're so sensitive. Now I can tell you the truth. I wouldn't like you to be frightened by something dangerous.'

'By one Stone Age boy?' Daniel said.

'You've dreamt about him too?' Madge said patronisingly. 'This is really interesting. Both of you now.'

'No, *seen* him,' Daniel said too quickly for Johnny to stop him.

Madge's expression changed. His face became more alert. His eyes darted from one to the other. All he'd cared about was whether they'd said anything to the men. 'Both of you?'

'Me for only a second. But Johnny – '

'You have, I can see you have!' Madge said. 'I was wrong, I never thought you would. But what did you see?'

Johnny shook his head at Daniel.

'You told me yesterday up the wood you'd seen nothing else,' Madge said. 'Why?'

'We don't trust you,' Daniel said. 'You'd found the cave even before we went over there the second time. And then there were all your lies to frighten us away. Now we've seen the Stone Age boy you want to be all friendly.'

'But you haven't seen him, have you?' Johnny said to Madge. It had dawned on him. How Madge had got to know about Kaa without seeing him him was another matter, but he suddenly knew definitely that Madge hadn't seen him like himself and Daniel.

'Why yes, I certainly have,' Madge said hastily and trying to ignore what Daniel had said. 'But the necklace – what about that?'

'Is that what you were looking for on the hill yesterday?' Johnny asked.

'Yes,' Madge said. 'Now, listen. If you should get on its track, you will let me know, won't you?' Suddenly he seemed anxious, as if he was afraid he was about to lose something.

'So you can return it to Kaa?' Daniel said.

'I'd make it worth your while,' Madge said quickly to Johnny, but glancing at Daniel as if he wasn't sure what he'd meant.

Johnny's suspicions grew deeper and deeper. Money? How could money be involved in this? And the knowledge that Madge had been made anxious by knowing the boys had seen Kaa made him wonder more. 'What's in this for you?' he said accusingly. 'It's about time you told us instead of all your lies. Do you really mean to return it to Kaa?'

But they didn't have that out for someone else rustled down the bank through the bushes. Madge said quickly, 'Not a word to anyone. Promise,' and turned round to face whoever was coming.

It was Mr Butler. 'There you are,' he said. 'We're going back to the farm straightaway.' He looked inquiringly at Charles Madge.

Charles Madge stepped across to meet him, holding out a hand to be shaken. 'I'm Johnny's cousin,' he said. 'Well his father's second cousin really.'

'Ah yes,' Mr Butler said, not really concentrating. 'Johnny did say his family had a visitor. Haven't I seen you up on the hill?'

'You may have done once or twice,' Madge replied nonchalantly. 'Have you got some kind of trouble? I saw all the activity from the house.'

'An odd kind of plant disease,' Mr Butler sighed. 'Trust me

and my farm to have to entertain it. Which reminds me – we really must be going, Daniel. They've packed up already. Are you coming too, Johnny?'

Johnny nodded.

'Goodbye then,' Madge said. 'And remember not to be too late, Johnny. We're all going out after lunch. That's what I really came down for – to remind you.'

He turned and had soon disappeared from view along the overgrown towpath.

'What's that you're standing by?' Mr Butler said to Daniel. 'There–by your foot.' He came and crouching down gazed at the wolf's print in the mud. 'My! That's large. What kind of dog made that?'

Johnny and Daniel exchanged a glance. Now was their chance to tell Mr Butler about Kaa.

'A large dog at any rate,' Mr Butler went on. 'Larger than any I know that's kept around here.'

Suddenly there was shouting from the field above. They were calling for Mr Butler.

'Something sounds urgent,' Mr Butler said. He straightened up. 'Perhaps they're onto something at last.' He cast a final look at the paw-print. 'Odd that.' The shouting grew louder. 'I'd better go,' he said. 'Worry about large dogs later. Perhaps it had something to do with the sheep being upset a couple of days ago.'

When the two boys were up with the rest in the sunny field above one of the men stoppd them. 'It's not your Dad's week,' he said to Daniel. 'I shouldn't go any closer if I were you. There's obviously a sheep-worrier on the loose. A nasty business.'

'Why, what's happened?' Daniel said anxiously, trying to peer past him.

'Some brute of a dog killed one of the sheep,' Mr Butler told him. 'It half ate it too. That's strange. It must have been really hungry. They usually kill for the sake of it.' As he stepped away from it Johnny and Daniel could see that behind the men lay a mangled sheep's carcass. 'Now I'll have to keep the animals near the farm. What luck!' He looked very angry. 'And if you've never heard of this disease – ' he gestured at the canal below for the Ministry of Agriculture men's benefit, 'how are you going to stop it?'

'We'll do what we can,' Mr Butler's friend said. 'We're all giving up our Saturday as it is.'

'I know you are, I know you are. I'm sorry. I'm just worried, that's all,' Mr Butler apologised.

'He saw the wolf-print, and now this. He'll believe us, I'm sure, about Kaa and the rest,' Daniel whispered to Johnny.

'Yes,' Johnny said. 'And we'll tell him about Madge too. We'll tell him everything. If only I didn't have to go out this afternoon. All three of us could start searching for the necklace straightaway.'

'At least Charles Madge is going with you' Daniel said. 'That gives him less time to search. And be careful with him, Johnny. I think that underneath he's even worse than I imagined.'

Johnny got another glimpse of the sheep and what the wolf had done to it. He had a sudden uncontrollable desire to be sick.

14

There was no way Johnny could get out of the afternoon's expedition. Madge managed to though. At the last moment he pleaded pressure of work.

He sauntered round five minutes after the family had arrived home. It was much too late for Johnny to go down to the farm again.

'Had a nice time?' he asked, easing himself into a chair in the back room and drawing on a cigarette. 'I'm truly sorry I couldn't come. It would have been interesting to have met Aunt Harriet, and I've not been out with you as a family yet.'

'Plenty of time for that if you're staying all summer,' Dad said. 'Your writing gone okay, Charles?'

'Fine, fine. I feel I'm really beginning to get to grips with it now.'

'We stopped off at a pub for a drink outside on the way back, which is why we're so late,' Mum explained.

'You should have rung. I'd have had time to come out to join you,' Madge said. 'English beer is a revelation after being brought up on Australian all my life.'

'Not something I could comment on,' Dad said. 'You lucky people who travel all over the world!'

'Now, don't go wandering off!' Mum called to Johnny who was gazing out over Denver from the back door. 'Bed time's very close.'

'I'm going upstairs a minute,' Johnny mumbled. He felt

utterly disgruntled. The day had started so excitingly; the rest had been sheer anti-climax. And not only that – their going out had given Madge yet more chance to wander about Denver on his own.

In his bedroom Johnny went to the window to stare out at Denver. How would Mr Butler have taken his idea that the opening up of the cave and Kaa had caused the winter weather, and that finding the necklace and giving it back was going to be the only cure for the experts' 'disease'? Johnny had left this morning before Daniel had had a chance to speak to his father on his own. It was so important that Mr Butler did take them seriously – he would be someone else, an older person, to help them find the necklace; and an ally in making sure Madge didn't get to it first.

The empty fields – Mr Butler seemed to have moved all his animals nearer the farm – were darkening by the time Johnny left the window. Where was the necklace, and would they or Madge find it first? That was the most important question for Johnny, for Kaa, and for Mr Butler too if only he knew it.

Downstairs he found Madge still there, in the sitting room watching television. He didn't look up as Johnny passed the open door though he was aware of Johnny passing by. Johnny sensed it. Probably he was wondering, just like Johnny, how much the other knew and how much he was keeping back.

Dad was in the kitchen. 'Time for bed?' he asked.

'Just about,' Johnny said.

'Anything wrong?' Dad asked, though not insistently. 'Something on your mind? You've looked a bit off-colour all afternoon. Worried about Mr Butler's farm? They'll clear that up – you'll see.'

'No, not that,' Johnny said. 'Just a bit tired.'

'Better off in bed then,' Dad said. 'Tomorrow's another day.'

Johnny was fetching biscuits for his supper when Charles Madge came into the kitchen too. Seeing him out of the corner of his eye, Johnny started. But he was only on his way to the back door. Johnny wondered whether he would have tried to wheedle more information out of him if Dad hadn't been there.

'I must get some more work done on my book before I go to sleep,' he said. 'Goodnight everyone. I'll see you tomorrow.'

'Goodnight,' Dad said. 'We won't disturb you, though how you can work at this time of night I don't know. I've heard you at the latest hours when I've had to slip out the back for something.'

Johnny said nothing.

'Goodnight, Johnny,' Madge repeated. The expression on his face seemed to ask: why aren't you being more friendly? Though of course the expression was more for Dad's benefit. Madge must be well aware what suspicious thoughts Johnny had in his mind about him by now.

Dad was taken in. 'Why so rude?' he said when the door was closed and Charles Madge had passed the kitchen window. 'I thought you liked your cousin. I certainly do. You just ignore him at the moment.'

'I didn't mean to be rude,' Johnny said untruthfully.

'You manage to be,' Dad replied angrily. 'Try and do something about it tomorrow.'

Up in bed Johnny could hear Charles Madge typing away. The noise as well as his own thoughts kept him wide awake. Charles Madge always typed at this time and Johnny always fell asleep before he finished, but tonight the sound got in the way of his thoughts. He would have liked to have talked to Madge, as Madge no doubt would have liked to talk to him, but in ideal circumstances, such as in front of Mum or Dad – or, even better, Mr Butler.

Soon it was no use trying to get to sleep. Johnny opened his eyes, then sat up in bed, got out and went to the window.

It was dark now, but a full moon lit up Denver hill and the whole valley. Johnny thought he could see more clearly than in daylight the track he and Daniel had followed over the top. There was not a light anywhere. To look now it might be anywhere in time, not in the twentieth century. Then he looked down into the two gardens. Everthing there was silvered with moonlight.

Eventually he went back to bed, but he hadn't been in it five minutes when he heard the click of Charles Madge's back door being opened and shut. Johnny sat straight back up in bed.

The strange thing was that the typing hadn't stopped! How could Charles Madge have opened and shut the back door while he was typing at the same time? He couldn't have. But Johnny hadn't heard anyone knock at the door and no one had come up the garden path. Someone had gone straight in without even bothering to knock and Madge hadn't minded. He must have been expecting his visitor if he hadn't even stopped typing . . .

Johnny listened, really puzzled. The typing went on without a moment's let up. Who was Madge's visitor? Johnny got out of bed and went to listen at his bedroom door. Both Mum and Dad were still downstairs. He heard their voices clearly. 'Come on, the serial's starting in a moment,' Mum was calling to Dad. 'I'm coming,' Dad called back. Johnny heard the lounge door being closed and the sound of the television suddenly went muffled and far away.

Who was Charles Madge's visitor?

It didn't take Johnny much time to make up his mind. He felt he had a responsibility. Here might be the clue to everything he was looking for, a way of finding out exactly what Madge was up to. He wanted the necklace – he knew that much. But what for, if not to give it back to Kaa? Perhaps Madge was working with someone else. In a moment Johnny had pulled his clothes on top of his pyjamas and was on the landing with his shoes in his hand. With great care he padded down the stairs. Luckily the carpet muffled any sound he might have made and luckily too he was pretty sure neither Mum nor Dad would come out. They looked forward to watching this television programme every week.

Johnny reached the bottom of the stairs and the sound of the television got louder. He took a deep breath and scurried past the lounge door into the kitchen. He hesitated at the door. Getting out was easy enough, but what if he couldn't get back in? Dad had left the key in the door. What if he turned it before Johnny got back? But he would have to take that chance, and if he found anything out it would be worth the trouble he'd get into. As quickly as he could he opened the back door and stepped outside into the night.

It was bright outside in the moonlight, a sharper more definite light than sunlight. Johnny quickly got his shoes on. He could hear the sound of typing again. It went on as regularly as ever. If Charles Madge's visitor was still in there, Charles Madge could not have stopped typing more than a moment to talk to him. Things were getting odder and odder.

Johnny stepped over the little fence that separated the two gardens and stood right next to Charles Madge's window. There was a broad chink in the curtains where they'd been drawn carelessly. Johnny edged up to it, crouching beneath the window-sill, then gradually eased himself up. He could see in now, though only part of the room was visible from his angle of vision. However there was no one there he could see. The visitor must be on the other side of the room, where the table and typewriter were, and which Johnny couldn't see from his present position. He ducked down under the window-sill again, eased along, then very carefully stood up and looked in again. He had a shock. Not only was there no visitor to see, there was no Madge either. Yet on the table the typewriter was typing away all by itself.

Johnny was fascinated. He forgot to take any precaution against being spotted. He pushed his face right up against the window and squinted in from every angle. The typewriter was acting as if someone was really there. There was no paper in it, but the keys were going up and down as if someone invisible was striking them. As Johnny watched the typing stopped and after several moments restarted. If someone had been listening but couldn't see (the position Johnny had been in every night till now), it would have seemed that a sheet of paper was being changed.

Johnny was shocked at first, but the shock didn't last too long. It didn't take much to work out that Charles Madge must have some clever device that made the typewriter work automatically. But why go to all this trouble? The answer was obvious and upsetting. Charles Madge must have gone to Denver. The click at the door had been him leaving and not someone coming in. He must have sneaked off there in the dark, careless about being noisy as he left tonight and forgetting to draw the curtains properly. He had got too confident. Perhaps he had sneaked off like this every night.

The typewriter typed on. Its keys rose and fell without anyone hitting them.

Whatever Charles Madge's game was, Johnny's job must be to stop him. There was nothing he could do tonight but perhaps if he went inside he would still learn something that would help foil him. After a brief glance around the garden Johnny opened Charles Madge's back door and very quietly stepped inside. Most people wouldn't have approved of what he was doing, but Johnny knew he was right. Madge was even more organized than he'd thought. Kaa was in danger from such a man who, without seeing Kaa, seemed to know more about him than Johnny did.

Johnny pulled the door to behind him, though he didn't like having to. He was quite confident there was no one inside, but even before Charles Madge had come he'd thought the house was creepy. Now it felt ten times more creepy with the typewriter working away on its own.

Johnny walked through to the living-room and looked around, eyes roaming everywhere. He wasn't sure at all what he wanted, nor what there was to find. After a moment he went to the desk and watched the typewriter keys rising and falling. There was a thick sheet of paper wrapped right round the roller that of course didn't need to be changed. No wonder Madge had so politely insisted no one ever interrupted him after he'd retired to write for the night. Then Johnny quickly opened the drawers of the desk. There was only blank paper, nothing else, no sign of the book Madge was supposed to be writing. The rest of the room was bare except for the book case. Johnny shut the drawers and went to look at Madge's reading.

Johnny recognised a number of library books from town. The spines of some of the older ones were marked 'Special

Collection. Not to be Borrowed,' which meant either that Madge had taken them out against the rules or that he'd managed to get special permission. All the library books were about the Summerfield and Yonderley districts. Then there were other books which had nothing to do with where Johnny lived. These must be Madge's own. They had titles like 'An A to Z of Ghosts in Britain', 'Actual Ghostly Happenings' and 'Ghosts: Facts and Fictions'. Johnny took one of them down. It was full of page-long paragraphs that gave Johnny no desire to read them, but in the middle there were pages of photos that were supposed to have been taken of ghosts, photos of equipment for detecting ghosts, and pictures of houses and places where ghosts were supposed to appear.

It seemed to Johnny absolutely clear that Madge had come here on false pretences. He hadn't come to visit the family or write a book at all. He'd come here because of Kaa. His interest in the district was confined to the wintry wood at Yonderley, Denver hill . . . and the necklace.

Johnny was just turning away when his eye caught sight of a piece of paper sticking out of one of the books. He took the book down and opened it up. The piece of paper was obviously being used as a book-mark. 'The Something or Other Canal' was the title of the book. It was old-looking, but it must have belonged to Madge for there were no library stamps on it.

Johnny was about to put it back when one of the words on the piece of paper suddenly had a meaning for him. *Psychic*. Mrs Braithwaite had used that word when the children had all written their stories about Kaa.

The piece of paper was the torn off heading from a letter. 'The World Wide Psychical Research Society' was embossed across the top and there was an address in London. Then he read the date: 6th July. *Dear Charles*, the letter started, *Thank you for your letter concering the talisman you believe you have located. Such a talisman would, as you realise, have a certain interest for us. However the price you suggest, should you obtain it, is, we feel, much too high. Who can know whether it will have the special powers you claim for it? We must discuss* . . . The letter was torn off here.

Talisman. Johnny didn't know what a talisman was but he felt sure it had something to do with Kaa and the necklace. But it was the date that staggered Johnny most. The sixth of July was days before Charles Madge was supposed to have arrived in England. He had told Johnny's parents that he had come straight to them from the airport. But all the time he'd been somewhere in England.

All of a sudden the typewriter stopped typing. Johnny darted back to it. He expected it to start again but it seemed to have gone quite dead now. It was electric. Then Johnny caught sight of the gadget on the socket that he'd noticed the night Madge had first talked with him. He knelt down by it and had a closer look, without touching it. It looked very delicate, like the insides of a transistor radio. When he stood up, withut warning the light went off. It was bad enough to be left in the dark, but a moment later the stairs light clicked on, and then the bathroom light. A moment later the taps in the bathroom began running and the toilet flushed. Yet no one had touched these things. Johnny stood there unable to move, rigid with fright. At the same time the grandfather clock in the hall was striking eleven.

There was still no one in the house apart from him, he was sure of that. Yet all of this had happened. It had happened automatically. To anyone listening from outside or from next door it would have seemed that Charles Madge was still there in the house. Only Johnny knew that he wasn't. But did it mean Madge would be back in a second?

Johnny knew how it had all happened. There was no magic and nothing ghostly involved, but suddenly he didn't want to be in the house any more. He had managed to scare himself in the past just by staring in through the windows! He replaced the book as best he could in the dark, rushed out of the back door and jumped across the little fence into his own garden. A solitary car was coming up the lane and Johnny stood stock-still by the back door as its lights passed across him. When it had gone he put his hand on the kitchen door-handle. Then he realised the car lamps had lit up something wrong. The door to the potting-shed had been standing partially open. Johnny had quite definitely bolted it earlier this evening.

Cautiously but quickly, for his parents' programme must be close to finishing soon, Johnny went down the path, over the fence again and round to the shed door.

Inside there was no bike. It had been stolen. So this was how Madge got to the canal at night! He had no need to use the Land Rover, and no questions were asked about where he went after dark. It allowed him to come and go as he wanted. Johnny remembered the tell-tale wisps of grass he'd found in the spokes yesterday but not bothered about at the time. Without meaning to he had aided Madge. He felt furious.

Johnny was almost half-way back to the kitchen door again when an animal howled from the valley below.

Kaa's wolf.

A dog answered it from the village, but it was more a howl of fear than a challenge. Suddenly Johnny felt his own back garden was full of dangers. He rushed for the door.

15

The phone rang next morning about eight. Johnny didn't hear it, but Dad did. Still more asleep than awake he came to fetch Johnny. 'It's Daniel,' he boomed in his early morning voice. 'I suppose he must think it's urgent. He doesn't use the thing more than once in a blue moon.' He yawned. 'Come on. Don't keep the lad waiting. He might come hammering on the back door and I couldn't stand that. Doesn't he know it's Sunday?'

'That you at last?' Daniel said at the other end of the phone. 'What do you do all the time in your house – sleep?'

'It's Sunday,' Johnny said as explanation. He tried to rub the sleep from his eyes and concentrate on Daniel's voice, very loud and fresh and wide-awake in his ear. 'We stay in bed. What's up?'

'What isn't up?' Daniel shouted, or it seemed to Johnny he shouted. 'Get dressed and get down here straightaway and I'll tell you.'

'No, tell me now,' Johnny said. He hadn't remembered the reason yet for another tiring night, but he definitely knew there was one, and he wanted to put things right by going back to sleep for as long as possible. 'Surely you can tell me over the phone. No one's eavesdropping.'

'We weren't here last night! Denver went back in time,' Daniel said. 'Dad thinks it was Kaa's time.'

Johnny remembered creeping next door last night and all he'd found out there; and then the howl of a wolf from the valley below, a real wolf.

'You weren't there?' he said. 'You went back in time?' He tried to take it in.

Daniel went on regardless. 'We couldn't see Summerfield last night, only a bare hill. Everything except the farm buildings had disappeared. Are you listening, Johnny? Just think what that means. Maybe, *if* we find the necklace, we'll be able to contact the real Kaa.'

'I'm coming,' Johnny said and put the receiver back.

'Dad!' He called softly to his parents' bedroom door. 'I'm going down Daniel's straightaway. I'll post the keys back through the front door letter-box. Okay?'

'Mmm!' came Dad's muffled reply which Johnny took to mean yes. He didn't stop to find out differently.

In the shed the bike was back in its place and the door bolted as it should be. Johnny glanced up and could see that Madge was still in bed like his parents. At least all the house curtains were drawn and the chink of open curtain that had betrayed Madge had been put right now. Madge would get no chance of borrowing the bike tonight – Johnny would rather hide it in a hedgerow somewhere than have that happen. Then he was away down the lane in the warm sun to the Butlers'.

The weather had gone back in time. It seemed logical Denver itself should too.

'I was the first to see it,' Mrs Butler said. 'It was a bit after six. I was gazing up the hill at Summerfield past our trees thinking about all that had happened yesterday – the Ministry of Agriculture men coming in the morning, then my husband and his friend and Daniel going over to Yonderley in the afternoon after Daniel had told them about your theory. Suddenly I couldn't believe my eyes. Summerfield had gone and the trees down our drive. There were just a few trees dotted about to the bottom of the valley, then bare hillside. I ran out of the kitchen to the back part of the house. The same had happened there. It had all changed and it was worse if anything. No fields any more, just pine trees pressing right up to the house. I rushed back to the front of the house. I thought I was going mad.'

'I'd noticed it by then,' Mr Butler said. 'I was out in the yard with Daniel. Some instinct made me glance towards the gate. It just wasn't there. Nor was anything on that open side of the yard. There were pine trees up the hill with a vague sort of track leading up between them. Up the hill where Summerfield should have been there was nothing. Only the hill.'

'What had happened?' Johnny said. 'What Daniel said on the phone?'

'We can only guess,' Mr Butler replied, 'but I think we went back – '

'In time,' Daniel said triumphantly. 'I told you.'

'We'd gone back in time like the weather on this hill has recently,' Mr Butler went on, 'to what it was thousands of years ago, whenever this Stone Age lad Daniel's told me about existed. The house and farm buildings were in a little clearing of this year – *now* – nineteen hundred and whatever it is. Instead of its just being the weather, the hill went back physically too. Summerfield Hill looked like man had never trodden on it.'

'And then?' Johnny asked breathlessly, for Mr Butler had paused.

Mr Butler laughed and frowned at the same time. 'I'm glad you're believing us,' he said, 'and I think you're the only person in the world at this moment, except for an odd crank or two, who would! As to what happened then, to be quite frank I panicked! Utterly! I bundled Daniel back into the house and found his mother as bewildered as myself. I tried the telephone. Dead as could be. No electricity, no radio – and that's run off batteries, so no sound waves were getting through – no television. Nothing twentieth century was working. So there we were, stuck firmly in the middle of a prehistoric world. I rushed round all the upstairs windows, but as far as I could see everything except the house and some of the out-buildings had gone. It was an eerie feeling, I can tell you. I hadn't the faintest idea whether it was just us or if it had happened to everyone. All the time I kept thinking – hoping really – it was a hallucination, something to do with what we'd seen during the day. I kept wondering whether to try getting the Land Rover down the track to see how far it went – if it did stop anywhere – but then I was worried about getting stuck and not being able to get back to the house. And what if the whole hillside changed back to our times while I was away? Where would I be left – back in the past?

'We sat in the kitchen looking out for ages and hoping things would change,' Mr Butler went on. 'It got darker and darker, and colder too. I went out one to make sure the animals were alright and fetch a storm-lantern from the barn. There was nothing about – animals, birds, anything – it was so still and quiet it was unbelievable. Outside, where it had changed back I mean, there was a regular breeze blowing, but we didn't feel it. It was like we were in a sealed-off bubble. My wife found some candles and when it grew pitch-dark we lit them and the lantern to give us some comfort. We lit the fire in the front-room, locked and bolted every door and window and settled down in armchairs in front of the fire for the night.'

'And what next?' Johnny said.

'Sometime in the night it must have changed back.' Mr Butler looked thoughtful. 'I can't say when. I went to have a look from the kitchen windows about four this morning and there was a light shining up in Summerfield, just a glimmer through the trees – *our* trees. I tried everything then – the lights, the radio, the phone.'

'And they all worked?' Johnny asked.

'A treat!' Mr Butler said. 'You can't guess how glad I was!'

'You believed us about Kaa,' Johnny said later, after he'd got through one of Mrs Butler's breakfasts. 'I wasn't sure you would.'

'Well, I didn't, not at first,' Mr Butler replied, 'though it added up somehow – the cold, the wolf I'd thought was a large dog, the ghost at the farm that frightened the animals, your dreams as well. After we'd got the sheep and cattle into fields near the farm Daniel persuaded me to go over to Yonderley. We took that friend of mine, the plant expert, since he was staying over for dinner, and what we saw just about confirmed what you and Daniel had worked out.'

'Dad's friend found Stone Age tools and ornaments in the cave,' Daniel said. 'Stone Age people had lived there.'

'But there was no necklace?' Johnny said. For a moment he'd hoped the Butlers had kept the good news back to surprise him with.

Mr Butler shook his head. 'No such luck. In any case your Australian cousin had got there first – the spade and pickaxe you'd seen him carrying were for digging up the cave floor. What we found he'd left. Some of the things were really nice and probably valuable too – three little ornamental things with rough carvings on, and some flints that might have been spear-heads. Or at least my friend says so. He's always been interested in archaeology, in fact he's spent more than one holiday on digs.'

'Some of them might have been Kaa's things!' Johnny said.

'Quite possibly,' Mr Butler agreed. 'What puzzles me, though, is why your cousin should have left those things he'd found and be so concerned about this necklace.'

'He's got a buyer for the necklace,' Johnny said. 'That's the reason. I would have told you sooner except your news put it out of my head.'

'But I thought Madge wouldn't tell you anything,' Daniel said.'

'He didn't tell me. I broke into his house last night!'

'Broke in!' Daniel said. 'You didn't!'

Briefly Johnny told them about his last night's adventure and the letter from the World Wide Psychical Research Society offering Madge money for a 'talisman'.

'A talisman?' Daniel said. 'Have you got that word right?' He turned to his father.

'A talisman's a ring or stone or anything like that that's meant to be magic or bring luck to whoever's got it,' Mr Butler said.

'Your instinct was right, Johnny – he is looking for the necklace, and he mustn't get it – we need it, I'm convinced of that now. Special powers, though – that must mean magic. Magic's one thing I don't believe in, but I suppose a magic object that once belonged to a priest would have considerable interest to someone who does believe in it.'

'Madge will find it if he goes on searching long enough,' Daniel said anxiously. 'We ought to start looking now, straightaway. There are four of us to his one.' He even got up.

Mr Butler shook his head. 'Not so fast,' he said. 'I may be completely wrong, but I think that what Johnny's cousin is doing is a waste of time. He's looking for a needle in a haystack, a needle in several dozen haystacks; and in any case that necklace is likely to be several feet under the earth by now if it's still on the hill. And that's no use to us. What is more, even if we dared risk going over the hill, it might change back any time and we'd get caught in the middle of it.'

'What then?' Johnny said. He'd half-risen with Daniel. 'Where do we look if not up the hill?'

'Perhaps a museum might have it, that's my only idea so far,' Mr Butler suggested. 'My friend might know. As I said he's well up on local archaeology. It may even be in a private collection somewhere in the vicinity. But until we find it we're just going to have to sit tight and hope your cousin doesn't find it first. I've a feeling we're going to be lucky though. Don't ask me how or why, but there seems to be some special connection between you and this Stone Age lad – Kaa you call him, isn't it? That's what I base my hopes on.'

Then Daniel shouted out.

'The window! Look!'

Johnny leapt up to look outside.

He saw for himself now what he'd only heard described so far. He held his eyes shut, not wanting to believe what he saw or rather didn't see. When he did open them there was no home, no Summerfield on the hill. Denver had gone back in time again.

Summerfield Hill stood bare and stark against a grey sky.

Half a dozen stunted pines were the only things growing on it. The farm and some of its outbuildings stood in a marshy-looking clearing ringed by trees, pine trees again. The faint line of a path seemed to run along the side of the clearing. Up the hill towards the top of Denver was dense pine forest.

'How long is it going to last this time?' Mr Butler said softly.

'It looks so cold and lonely,' Mrs Butler said. 'So bare and desolate. It's incredible to think people survived there once.'

Kaa's country!

Johnny stared out at it.

'I wonder if Kaa's out there?' he said slowly as the idea took hold of his mind.

16

'Seen Charles today?' Dad was saying over his shoulder to Mum as Johnny came up the garden path about midday that morning. He was reading the paper on the back doorstep, shirt off and improving his tan.

'Not yet,' Mum called back. 'He can't be up yet. He seems to have caught the English late Sunday morning habit with a vengeance today.'

'Here's Johnny,' Dad called. 'Johnny, are Uncle Charles' curtains drawn? I can't be bothered to go and look again.'

'Still closed,' Johnny said.

'Perhaps I'd better go and give him a knock,' Dad said, though without moving a muscle to do so. 'Oh – ' he yawned. 'This sun makes me lazy.'

'I noticed,' Mum said. 'Ask if Johnny's had anything to eat yet. I still don't know what you were doing letting him out so early on a Sunday.'

'I've eaten,' Johnny called, still gazing at the curtained windows next door. Why were they still closed? Wasn't Charles Madge going out searching today? He hadn't found the necklace, had he? He couldn't have – Mr Butler had said the chances against that were millions to one. But there was always the possibility . . .

Johnny turned to look at Denver. The change at the farm this time had only been for half an hour, not half the night, but he'd been in it, he'd experienced it. The view of where he stood now had been bare and windswept. The continuous clouds in the sky had held snow. Johnny shuddered. He couldn't conceive it, so chill and hostile the landscape had been; nor could he conceive how two times had managed to exist at once, so that to people in Summerfield Denver had looked normal. There must exist some point, Mr Butler thought, where you passed over from present time into past, corresponding, he guessed to the boundary of the ancient wood.

'What are you staring at?' Dad said. He put aside his paper as Johnny tore his eyes away from Denver. 'The hill, is it? Those woods at the top look as if autumn's hit them in this light, the trees around the canal cutting too. I was thinking of wandering down to have a look, it's so strange. Any more news from those scientists who were swarming around the Butlers' place yesterday?'

'They say it's a disease of some kind,' Johnny said. 'They're coming back tomorrow or Tuesday to spray the trees I think.'

'That'll cheer Mr Butler up, then,' Dad said. He stared at Denver several seconds, obviously deeply puzzled by it all, then stood up.

'Be a good lad and give your Uncle a knock,' he said. 'I'm just going to get a book that might interest you. I remembered it last night after you'd gone to bed. It was in the spare-room in a trunk. Oh, and be polite to Uncle Charles,' he called over his shoulder. 'Remember what you promised.'

Johnny obeyed. He went over the low fence and knocked at Madge's door, then stood well away from it, not trusting Madge. There was no answer. He knocked again harder and there was still no answer.

'Is Charles Madge's Land Rover out the front?' he said to Mum as he went through the kitchen. 'I couldn't make him hear if he's in.'

'It was half an hour ago, and here's dinner nearly ready,' Mum said in exasperation. 'Everyone's time seems topsy-turvy today. And why can't you call your cousin Uncle Charles – I'm sure he'll think Charles Madge is impolite.'

'There you are,' Dad said, emerging from the back room. He

had a book in his hand. 'This should interest you. The canal – '

'Canal?' Johnny said, jumping at the mention of it. 'What about the canal?'

'It's a history of it, that's all. It shouldn't be too hard for you.' Johnny's face dropped at the prospect of reading the ancient-looking volume held out to him. But it was better than his Dad having found out the real reason for his interest in the canal. 'I haven't read it for years, but they had an interesting time of building it, especially the tunnel if I remember rightly. If you're going to go exploring such places you might as well find out something about them,' Dad finished. 'You shouldn't entirely waste your holidays.'

'Thanks, Dad,' Johnny said, trying to sound more grateful than he was. He dropped the book off in his room on his way to wash his hands and use the bathroom. It might help to pass the time one day when the present excitement was over. He didn't even stop to look at the title.

Dad knocked and called again, but no Madge emerged from next door so they had dinner without him. Mum kept something hot in the oven. There was no explanation. The Land Rover was still out the front. 'Perhaps he stayed up working very late,' Dad said. 'He says he's really getting his teeth into this book he's working on. I heard him moving about around four this morning and I thought he'd got up to go to the bathroom. Perhaps he'd only just finished work at that time.'

Johnny said nothing, but he knew where Madge had just got back from at that time of the morning. He must have been there during the time-change. No wonder he was tired!

The day turned out sultry. The sky over Denver darkened, though it was bright over the village at the front of the house. Mum and Dad thought it would rain, though Johnny knew that Denver had its own kind of weather now. Where was the necklace? Mr Butler was right – Madge couldn't have it, even the most systematic search of Denver wouldn't find it. But find it Johnny had to. Hadn't Kaa's father said he would? But where and how? He felt so useless just sitting and waiting.

'Going down to Daniel's later?' Dad asked as Johnny got up from table. 'We don't seem to see much of you nowadays. Couldn't you two stay up here?'

'Later perhaps.' It wasn't that he didn't want to go down or that he was scared to, but Mr Butler had said he wasn't to. If it was absolutely necessary Mr Butler would come and fetch him in the Land Rover. Mr Butler was worried about what would happen if Johnny wandered onto Denver during a time-change.

Johnny went upstairs and perched in his usual place at the window, eyes glued to the hill. Though where he sat was in the sun, the whole of Denver was in shadow and the sky over it seemed to be going darker still. Johnny had a sudden thought – was a time-change happening down there this very minute? There was no way of telling from outside. If so he ought to be there, whatever Mr Butler said. Mightn't he be meant to go back in time and find the necklace? He would sneak down after tea and hide himself in one of the out-houses of the farm till things changed. Then, who knew? He threw himself down on the bed in exasperation and in doing so hit his shoulder on Dad's book which he'd completely forgotten. He pushed it to one side, then to distract himself took it up and opened it. Dad would ask if he'd read it, so he might as well look.

He opened it at random. The print was small and there were no pictures. This page was about digging the canal at some place he'd never heard of. He began flicking through and was about to put it down again when the name Denver Hill caught his eye. It took him a moment to refind the place, and what he saw made him start searching back through the pages to the beginning of the passage. This took him to the start of a chapter entitled *The Tunnel At Denver Hill.*

Half-way through his reading Johnny heard Madge and Dad calling to each other and Madge explaining how late he'd been up, but even that didn't draw Johnny away from the book. What he was reading was in difficult language, but it was much too interesting for him to put down yet. And there was another thing about this book – it was the same one Madge had had on his shelf next door! This was the one way Madge, the outsider, could have known why to come to Yonderley and Summerfield, though it still didn't explain how he'd happened to be here at the right time.

The chapter began: 'Denver Hill lies roughly half-way between the two end points of the canal, and work reached there at the beginning of summer that year (about 1780 Johnny saw from the previous chapter). No way was found of avoiding this hill, which rises to some six hundred feet above sea level at its summit and which is covered at the top by an ancient wood which is mentioned for its game in Doomsday Book, and was only partially felled in 1896 on the Summerfield side. The Yonderley side is to this day in its prehistoric state as far as the wood is concerned. A person from before the time of Christ would probably recognise it now.

'Permission was gained from the landowner, the Earl of Baddley Green, and work began on the Summerfield side. After several locks the canal was laid up a little valley down which a stream ran, then after felling numerous trees work began on tunnelling. The chief architect, Mr Gregors, lodged at Summerfield Farm (presumably Mr Butler's farm now, Johnny thought) whose occupant farmed below the wood and had rights to the wood and its game. The farm lay in a natural clearing on the edge of the wood. Mr Gregors chose to make his headquarters this side, fearing trouble with springs in the rock, though none in fact occurred.

'Mr Gregors had soon to transfer his main attention to the Yonderley side of the hill. The land there has none of the steady if steep climb to the top of the hill on the Summerfield side. The canal was brought to its correct height from the valley by a series of twelve locks in close succession and here it faced an almost cliff-like side of the hill in a narrow valley. During the final work bringing the canal bed to the entry point for the tunnel, room had to be cleared on either side for workmen's huts, stockpiling materials and so on. In dynamiting away a spur of rock evidence was found of some ancient disaster, namely a skeleton of a man about five feet in height, almost perfectly preserved in the stone. The neck of the man (a doctor was called to examine it) appeared to have been broken by some animal to judge by the state of the bones. Many of the men began to mutter saying the whole thing was ill-luck and the place fated. The discovery of a cave nearby, its mouth covered by falls of rocks, did nothing to quieten these superstitious creatures, though indeed seeing what followed they may have been right to see an ill-omen in its discovery. Mr Gregors left a note in his diary of having gone into the cave himself. He wrote it was small and ill-lit and that it appeared to have been inhabited some considerable time in the past to judge by a flint spear-head and other small objects he found there and left.

'The ill-luck that dogged the tunnel appears to have started from the moment a lad less scared than the rest of his companions went into the cave for a bet. While inside he was heard to scream. It was thought he was joking, but after a while he had not emerged and one of the less fearful of his friends went in and hastily dragged him out. On recovering consciousness the boy declared, still in much fear, that while inside there had been a sudden flash of light and in front of him he had seen a strange-looking youth crouched over what seemed to be a dying man and speaking to him about something lost. Then, not able to stand the sight any longer, he had screamed and fainted.

'Nothing could shake the boy from his story, and eventually for the good of the canal Mr Gregors had him sent away to another job, though strange to say the boy was not afraid to stay after his initial shock. He began to tell stories about a boy who, he said, had once stayed in the cave and how he had needed help. He said he had heard in dreams that it was a magic necklace that had been lost thereabouts on the hill and needed to be returned to the ghostly boy. Mr Gregors ordered the cave to be blocked up and its entrance covered over with rocks and earth in order to try and calm the men, many of whom slipped away not to be seen again. Whether the architect believed in the boy's story I cannot say, but he did his best to conceal the cave for on visiting Yonderley myself I found no trace of it nor could the local inhabitants remember there ever having been such a cave.

'So the work slowly proceeded. In fact the tunnel itself being reasonably short and through good rock was little trouble in itself. The trouble lay not in the tunnel, though it took two long years to complete, but in the events that followed what the boy had claimed to have seen. A mysterious disease laid waste the whole wood on both sides of the hill, at Yonderley and at Summerfield, particularly in the regions of the cave and the farm on the other side. A cold hung over the hill and water froze in the middle of August. It snowed in September (Mr Gregors writes this in his diary himself) and overhead at the same time a clear sky! Workers and local people alike said they had seen a lone wolf in the woods, and the farm at Summerfield had particular trouble with its animals which were in a constant state of uproar. In fact the hill at times was so desolate people claimed they had wandered into another country. All this went on till the following spring. By then scarcely a worker remained from the original crew and replacement workers, when they could be found, did not stay long. At times there were so few labourers remaining that work ceased altogether. The following summer things returned somewhat to normal and it was possible to retain a more or less steady workforce, though there were reports of a shadowy wolf or wolves being seen still, and only on the Yonderley side the disease still raged and the cold lingered. By the following summer things were completely back to normal. Almost two years to the day after commencement of work the tunnel was opened, the canal filled with water and the first barge able to pass through. Meanwhile the delays due to the "Yonderley happenings" had caused considerable hardships to the canal company.

'I have inquired among the present-day inhabitants of Yonderley and Summerfield, but have found no memory of these events. Nor have I found the cave.'

Johnny threw the book down on the bed and jumped to the window. It might be his imagination but the autumnal colour was now visibly creeping along the hedgerows from the canal cutting towards the farm. Did this mean that Denver Hill and the Butlers' farm were in for two years of disaster?

'Claimed they had wandered into another country' – how near the people of those times had been to the truth!

Johnny went back to the book. It said no more, however, about the canal tunnel or the ghostly happenings – Johnny searched it end to end. Then quite naturally, for he'd had very little sleep last night and got up very early, he fell asleep with the book open at the index. His sleep was full of the landscape he'd seen this morning during the time-change. In it he searched among the frosted pines for the lost necklace, though it was a desperate search for the wolf was always near.

'Come on, Johnny,' Mum was saying when he next opened his eyes. 'Daniel's on the phone for you. What are you two up to that he's suddenly started making these important phone-calls?'

'What time is it, Mum?'

'Half past six,' she said. 'I've been up twice before, but you were dead to the world. I was going to wake you up anyway – you'll never sleep tonight at this rate.'

'The time-change lasted four hours this time,' Daniel said breathlessly down the phone. 'It only went back to normal a few minutes ago.'

'It all looked perfectly normal from up here,' Johnny said. 'It's strange, isn't it? Mum and Dad would have noticed if it had changed from here too.'

'I wish you'd have been here to see them,' Daniel said. 'We watched them for a good three or four minutes before they disappeared up into the pines on the hill. Then there was the wolf on their trail. It changed back soon after he went by.'

'Seen who?' Johnny said. 'I'm not with you. Them?'

'Kaa and his father!' Daniel said. 'I told you. It was about an hour and half ago. There were two people coming up the track, a boy our age in front and a man behind. We thought at first that some outsiders had ignored a notice board Dad put up to warn people to keep out, and blundered into the time-change. Then we saw they were dressed in furs, all ragged and long-haired. They had faces just like Eskimos, just like Kaa had in the cave that time we saw him.'

'Kaa and his father!' Johnny said. 'You saw them! If only I'd been there! Tell me – did they see you?'

'No! They walked right through where our barn ought to be but they didn't even glance our way. Then about half an hour after they'd disappeared we saw the wolf. Hang on a minute.'

Mr Butler came on the phone. 'You've heard all about it,' he said. 'We'll phone you again in the morning to tell you if anything else has happened and to let you know about going to look for the necklace. The more I think about it, the more likely it seems to me that if it's still in existence it's in a museum or a collection somewhere. I'm sorry to rush you, Johnny, but there's always the chance it may change back again and I've several phone calls to make. By the way,' he added, 'there was a journalist down here earlier firing off questions. It doesn't see likely that your cousin would want the press onto it so maybe one of the Ministry men who came yesterday got talking in the pub,' Mr Butler said. 'It's irritating, though. If his story does get put in the paper, that's sure to lead to some unwanted visitors. Johnny, about Kaa – I do wish you'd been here to see him – '

Suddenly Johnny was aware of stealthy movement behind him. Madge had come out of the kitchen and closed the door so quietly behind himself that Johnny had heard nothing.

'Goodbye, I'll see you tomorrow, Mr Butler,' he said into the phone and hastily slammed it down.

Then he turned to face Madge.

To judge by the look on his face Madge could have throttled Johnny at that moment.

Johnny and Madge faced each other. They were in the open now. Both knew which side he was on. And this was the first time they'd been entirely alone since meeting at the canal yesterday morning.

'I moved my bike so you couldn't use it again,' Johnny said. 'I know you're not in there typing at night *and* I saw a letter in one of your books saying why you want the necklace. You won't get it.'

'Say one word to your parents and I'll say several words that'll make sure you don't go near the Butlers or Denver in the near future,' Madge said, his eyes furious.

It was the only kind of bargain Johnny was prepared to strike with Madge.

The kitchen door opened again, more noisily this time.

Mum came out but Madge was already on his way to the toilet. All the same Mum's eyes flickered queerly from one to the other.

'All right?' Dad said when Johnny came into the kitchen. 'That's the second time Daniel's phoned today.'

'Yes, all right,' Johnny said.

Then it struck him.

If tonight had been the night Kaa and his father went over the hill, then tomorrow would be the night that the wolf came for Kaa. And the necklace had to arrive before the wolf did.

That meant he had fewer than twenty-four hours to find it . . .

17

The wind whistled eerily across the mouth of the cave. Outside darkness gathered and snow-laden clouds sailed low over the little valley.

Kaa sat cross-legged on the cave floor, his right hand gripping the shaft of his father's great spear, ready to lift and thrust. The wolf would come soon. Kaa knew there was no escape. He had to face it. The God had sent the wolf. It was fated.

Kaa had an aching longing for home, for his mother and sisters and for his village nestled in the hills far south of this forsaken place. He wished that his father had not been priest, that his father had been some simple ordinary hunter. It overwhelmed him, the knowledge that his father was dead and that he would be priest – if he could add the wolf's claws to the sacred necklace.

But first he must have the necklace itself. *Help*! *help*! Kaa's voice went out to the one who was to help.

Then, without knowing how, Kaa knew the one his father had spoken of with his dying breath would come. He knew that with certainty. The God had sent the knowledge. The one would come, though beyond that there was doubt and uncertainty. It was Kaa's first moment of priestly insight. He bowed his head to the ground in thanks.

Outside the wolf howled, though from far away. It must have circled off through the hills in search of game. The howl was a challenge to Kaa. He stood up in answer and walked to the cave mouth. In the sky darkness was gathering. There were two ways the wolf could come – up the valley and the rock-pile, or slithering down the cliff-face from above him. Kaa's eye avoided the spot among the rocks where earlier in the day he'd carried his father's body and covered it deep with stones . . .

. . . Johnny woke to the early morning light. He was instantly awake. Mum or Dad was running water in the bathroom and the pipes were singing, but it wasn't that that had woken him. It had been the wolf howl so clear in his ears that it might have been just down in the valley below.

The bathroom lock was opened with a snap.

'Did you hear that howl?' Johnny's sharp ears caught Dad call softly to Mum. 'What a noise.'

'I was just dozing off,' Mum complained. Her voice grew louder as she came out of the bedroom onto the landing. 'It sent the shivers up my spine. It must have woken half the people in the neighbourhood. What time is it?'

'A quarter to seven,' Dad said. 'My usual time. Early. Where was it, I wonder, that dog? It sounded almost in our back garden.'

'I thought it was somewhere on Denver,' Mum said.

Johnny got out of bed and parted the curtains. Denver lay dark and sullen, though the sun shone in Johnny's garden.

If Johnny was right, today was the day of decision for both him and Kaa.

Where was the necklace?

Dad was engrossed in the paper before setting off to work. This was a ritual Johnny didn't often see.

He stifled a yawn. His body wanted to be in bed, but his mind knew he had to be up to answer the phone.

'I'll get you something in a moment,' Mum said, settling down beside Johnny with a cup of tea. 'You *are* early.'

'It's all right, I can wait,' Johnny said.

The back door opened and through it came Charles Madge. The air he let in with him was cool but already smelt of sun. Today would be another scorcher, at least in Summerfield. Madge clumsily shut the door behind him. Johnny, giving him a quick glance, saw his eyes were puffy with lack of sleep. Who knew what time he had got in off Denver last night? Johnny, who had lain awake till after Mum and Dad had come to bed, had not heard him come in, though he'd heard him stealthily leaving just after the typewriter had started up. He would have had to walk too for Johnny had put the bike elsewhere.

'Morning, Charles,' Dad said, without lifting his eyes from the paper. 'Off to the library as usual?'

'Morning,' Charles Madge grunted. He glanced at Johnny as suspiciously as Johnny had looked at him, then ignored him.

'I can't say I feel too hot this morning,' he said, sitting down in the only remaining chair. 'Maybe I'll give it a miss today or go in later.'

(Johnny stirred. A change from his usual routine. Did Madge intend to hang about the house today? Why?)

'You should have stayed in bed,' Mum remarked sympathetically. 'What is it? A cold?'

'Just general tiredness,' Madge said. 'I feel a bit run-down.'

'Too many late nights,' Mum said.

The conversation died. Dad rustled his paper, Mum yawned and Madge and Johnny sat in silence.

'A proper cross-roads this kitchen is this morning,' Dad said, glancing over his paper at all and sundry. He laughed. 'I bet Johnny's not seen downstairs this early before in his life.'

'Anything special you got up for?' Madge said. His eyes darted at Johnny from under his puffy lids. 'Got something planned with Daniel?'

'No, nothing in particular,' Johnny said.

'You didn't go down to see him yesterday afternoon or evening, did you?' Mum said. 'That's unusual. Not quarrelled, have you?'

'Of course not!' Johnny snapped.

Dad turned over another page of his newspaper. 'How interesting,' he said. 'Something about Summerfield in here. Not often we get in the news.'

'What sort of thing?' Mum asked casually. 'Good news, I hope.'

'Hang on a minute,' Dad said, creasing back the paper to get at the article more easily.

Johnny sat up. He immediately knew what it was and Madge didn't – that was obvious from the way he still gazed out of the window.

'How extraordinary!' Dad said. 'It's about that trouble Mr Butler has at the farm. Apparently it's not just the farm it's affecting either. It spreads right over Denver and part of the way down the other side to Yonderley. Let me read it to you.' Dad glanced at his watch. 'I've just about got time.'

'A mystery plant disease has struck a remote farm on Denver Hill near Summerfield,' the article read. 'Ministry of Agriculture specialists visited the farm on Saturday but no identification of the disease has yet been made. All types of plant life are hit, and our reporter yesterday found trees in the major area of infection stripped of leaves and apparently dead or dying. In appearance at least they had been killed by the most severe of frosts, and in their vicinity it did indeed seem as if the temperature had been lowered by several degrees. Incredible at the start of what promises to be a record heatwave.

'Mr Butler, the farmer, declined to make a comment and has now put his farm out of bounds to all visitors. The disease has apparently occurred in the past in precisely this part of the world. A history of the canal that passes under Denver Hill states that it happened in the year 1780 and that the hill was laid waste for two years before all returned to normal. At the time the happening was associated with ghostly events, though today's experts will undoubtedly find more ordinary explanations.'

'Is that all?' Madge said rather sharply.

'Why yes,' Dad replied. 'There are two photos as well though. Have a look at them.' Madge had to restrain himself from grabbing the paper.

Dad glanced at his watch and got up. 'Better be going.

Monday's always a busy morning. You already knew quite a lot about this, didn't you?' he said to Johnny.

'Yes.'

'Well, goodbye all. I wish I had time to stay and talk about it.'

'Goodbye, Dad,' Johnny said.

Madge barely mumbled goodbye. He was too interested in the paper. He came round the table and thrust the paper under Johnny's nose. 'This *is* Daniel's father isn't it?' he said.

Johnny pushed the paper back to see it properly. There were two pictures – one of some devastated trees, apparently at the canal, but they could have been taken anywhere – then a picture of Mr Butler looking rather uncharacteristically irritated in front of the farm-house porch.

'You know it is,' Johnny said.

Mum glanced, but Madge took his rude tone easily.

'And where is he? Standing in front of his house?'

'Yes.' Then Johnny saw the look on Charles Madge's face. The sleep and tiredness had gone from his eyes. 'Why?' Johnny asked.

'That's what I thought,' Madge said, pursing his lips and ignoring the question. He took the paper back, scanned it one more time, then decisively put it folded on the table.

Johnny picked it straight back up and opened it at the photo. The photo of Mr Butler was clear as could be. The caption said who it was and Madge had already met Mr Butler. And there was the familiar porch. Then why . . .

'Don't bother about breakfast for me,' Madge was saying to Mum. 'I'll get something to eat in town.'

'But you can't go out on an empty stomach when you're feeling poorly!'

Mum protested but Madge was already half way out of the door. He just wasn't listening. In fact he was a revived man. He had woken up completely when he'd seen the photo. But why? Johnny scanned it again. There was just Mr Butler and the porch, Mr Butler was on the point of telling the photographer to put his camera down and go away, and the porch looked as it always did – a flowering plant growing up a trellis one side and a rusty horseshoe over the square lintel.

A minute later Johnny and Mum heard the Land Rover engine roar into life out front.

'He got better very quickly,' Mum said. She shook her head. 'He had breakfast here all last week and left later than this. Why the desperate hurry today? Now, what about you, Johnny? You're not going to turn my food down?'

'No, Mum,' Johnny said, but he hadn't much appetite either. It was the excitement of waiting for the Butlers to phone or, better still, just arrive. He wanted to hear everything about what they'd seen of Kaa and his father last night. If only he'd been down there to see him, he thought again.

Three quarters of an hour later the phone rang.

'You get it,' Mum said, but Johnny was already on his way. This had to be Daniel.

'Did anything else happen last night?' Johnny began saying regardless of whether Mum heard him or not, but Daniel cut him short.

'Your Australian cousin's been down here,' Daniel said. 'Dad had to virtually throw him off the farm.'

'He left here in a rush like he'd suddenly made his mind up to do something,' Johnny told him. 'What happened?'

'He must have parked his Land Rover out of sight down the drive. The first we saw of him he was behind the farm yard gate looking round. Then he climbed straight over the gate and was heading for the house when Dad ran out and stopped him. He kept going too even though Dad shouted at him. I thought there was going to be a fight for a moment.'

'Fight!' Johnny repeated, stupefied. 'But what for?'

'We don't know,' Daniel said. 'He wouldn't say anything. It seemed like he meant to sneak up to the house, but what he wanted to do when he got there, goodness knows.'

Then suddenly Johnny knew why Charles Madge had got better so quickly. 'Wait, Daniel. I won't be a moment,' he said, then put the phone down on the table. 'Where's the paper,

Mum?' he called as he ran into the kitchen.

'Paper?' Mum said. 'Where you left it.'

It was on the chair Dad had been sitting on for breakfast. Johnny spread it out on the breakfast table across all the as yet uncleared cups, saucers and plates. A glance at the picture of Mr Butler in front of the farmhouse porch was enough. Johnny had walked past and by the necklace ever since he'd first gone to the Butlers' – Daniel had lived with it all his life. It was hanging up on the porch wall, plain for all to see. It had always hung there. And Madge had been the one to spot it.

'Thanks, Mum,' Johnny said.

'What for?' she said.

'I know what he wanted!' Johnny shouted into the phone. 'And I'm coming down! Now!'

18

Kaa's necklace lay on the Butler's kitchen table, spread out in an oval on the scrubbed wooden surface, dozens of wickedly sharp claws strung painstakingly on a narrow leather thong. Kaa's necklace – but not Kaa's yet.

Johnny ran his finger tips along the claws, feeling their sharpness.

'What now then?' Daniel said excitedly.

'Give him time to think,' Mrs Butler said. 'So many things to take in and so early on a Monday morning.' She put the cup of tea she'd poured several minutes ago for Johnny into his hands and then glanced at the necklace herself – none of them could take their eyes off it. 'Though what you want him to say I'm not sure I want to know,' she said. 'I just hope it involves nothing dangerous.'

Johnny took a sip at the tea, then put the cup behind him on the dresser. The necklace attracted his glance again.

'It's a good luck charm that's been in the family for years, like the horseshoe you see on some folk's doors,' Mr Butler said. 'Come to think of it, we've got a horseshoe ourselves. But this necklace, I can't say I've even looked at it, let alone taken it down except years ago when I was a child.'

'I didn't even know it was there,' Daniel said. 'What a good job we spotted Charles Madge climbing over the gate.'

'My grandfather used to say they were tigers' claws brought back by some relation years back who ran away to sea, but that obviously can't be true. Mind you, as claws go they're large enough,' Mr Butler said.

'Yesterday I was in absolute despair. I never thought we'd find it,' Johnny said jubilantly. He picked the necklace up carefully as if it might break or turn to dust in front of his eyes – he still couldn't believe it was found. The thong, though, seemed strong enough. Where it had hung was sheltered and airy, Mr Butler said, which might account for the leather not having rotted, though he didn't think it could be the original. Probably whoever had found it had restrung it.

'Put it on, Johnny,' Daniel said.

Johnny hesitated and glanced at Mr and Mrs Butler.

'Even if Kaa thought it was magic, it can't be now,' Mr Butler said. 'Not for you.'

Johnny pulled the necklace over his head. At once, even more vividly than before, he got a sense of how old it was, how much it meant to Kaa. But no, it was not magical, at least not for him. For Madge's clients perhaps. At the thought of Madge Johnny said, 'He saw me coming down here. He was coming up the hill in the Land Rover as I left the house. He'll know I've guessed where the necklace is.'

'He's no reason to,' Mr Butler said.

'He has,' Johnny said. 'I'd just told him I had no plans to come down here today. He'll ask Mum why I rushed out. Mum'll tell him I came dashing in for the paper.'

'No matter,' Mr Butler said. 'I guess once we'd turned him off our land he'd have come straight to you trying to make some deal. At least we all know where we stand now. And *we* have got the necklace, even if I'm not sure what we're going to do with it.'

'What Johnny is going to do with it,' Daniel said. 'He ought to decide.'

'Yes,' Mr Butler agreed. 'You're right there. Well, Johnny? What do you plan to do with it?'

'It's going back,' Johnny said. 'To Kaa.'

'And how?' Mrs Butler asked anxiously.

Johnny gestured at the view through the window.

'When the right time-change comes,' he said. 'I've worked it out. Kaa went over the hill last night. The necklace has to go back to Kaa the second night he spends in the cave, and that's tonight.'

Mr and Mrs Butler looked at each other.

'We don't even know it's possible to pass over,' Mr Butler said. 'We can see the prehistoric hill when it changes, but does it exist? Can we touch it? Even if you did such a dangerous thing and went over the hill to the cave, when the time changes what guarantee have you got that this necklace existing now can be handed back to Kaa existing then?'

'Charles Madge was on the hill last night during the time-change and the night before, and he came back,' Johnny said. 'And anyway Kaa is waiting for it. If I don't take it, who will? I've got to go, haven't I, unless I'm going to let him down, and if I do let him down there will be two years of this weather on your land.'

'That book account – ' Mr Butler said. 'I wish in a way you'd never found it, then we wouldn't know the worse.'

'We're going with him,' Daniel said. 'Dad – we've got to.'

Mr Butler nodded. 'It's the maddest thing I've ever attempted, but yes, we'll try. We'll come up and fetch you in the Land Rover about half past four, Johnny. We'll approach the cave from the Yonderley end. It will make the journey we have on foot shorter. Then we'll wait and see.'

Johnny touched the necklace round his neck.

'And this,' he said. 'I think I ought to keep it. I know it's yours, but I think Kaa and his father would want me to look after it.'

'What about Madge?' Mr Butler said.

'*He* won't get it,' Johnny said.

The necklace felt heavy round Johnny's neck as he approached Charles Madge up the garden path some minutes later. His cousin had evidently decided (for Mum's benefit) that he was after all not up to his usual stint in the library, but he'd equally evidently not wanted to go and lie down. Instead, sporting a wide-brimmed sun-hat he was out smoking in a deck-chair with the paper in his lap and in a good position to keep an eye on what went on.

Approaching him Johnny toyed with the idea of telling Mum about the necklace and Madge's involvement with it, then dismissed the idea. If the whole story came out there would be no going over Denver this evening.

He meant to get past Madge without speaking, but Madge reached out a hand to bar his way.

'Found it, then, have you?'

'Thanks to you,' Johnny said, keeping his distance.

'I was right then. Who has it now? You or the Butlers?'

'The Butlers of course.'

Madge tipped his sun-hat back and studied Johnny's face. 'I'm not so sure,' he said. 'But that's by the way. I'm sure you can lay your hands on it if you want to. Listen – I can make it very worth your while to pass it over to me voluntarily because I mean to have it, Johnny.' He twisted in his chair and prised a wallet out of his back pocket. 'Look,' he said, opening it and pulling a wad of ten pound notes partly out to show him. 'I've had these ready for you, should you get there first. I realised there was the possibility. Silly of me to have encouraged you I suppose. I thought you might know something I didn't.'

'I don't want your money,' Johnny said. 'Now let me go past?'

'You don't realise what you're turning down. Johnny,' Charles Madge said. 'Who else is going to buy it off you? A museum? A collector? It won't fetch anything compared with what I'm offering you.'

'I know exactly what you want it for, and I don't want money for it,' Johnny said firmly.

'Why all the trouble then? Why get in my way?' Madge asked. He seemed genuinely at a loss. 'What do you mean to do with it? Donate it to a museum? What a waste.'

'Give it back to Kaa,' Johnny said. 'I thought you'd have realised that by now.'

'Kaa? You mean that boy you dreamt about and imagined you saw in the cave? You've got a name for him!' Madge laughed. 'And how do you intend to give it back to him?' Madge laughed again. '*Dream* it back to him? But you can't give it back to a ghost. You're wasting everyone's time, Johnny. Honestly you are.' He leant across, dropping the wallet as he did so, and touched Johnny on the far pocket where his handkerchief made it bulge. 'You do have it, don't you? I can feel it.' Johnny stepped further away and Madge got up. 'Or is it round your neck?'

'He's there, on Denver,' Johnny said. 'He went up the hill last night past the farm. Mr Butler and his family saw him. It's his, and I'm going to return it.'

Madge started.

'Kaa is real,' Johnny said, 'as real as you or me when the time changes back.'

Madge was silent for a moment. 'You don't know what it's like out there when it changes back,' he said grimly, 'nor your fine Butler friends. I've not met them on the hill sightseeing when it changes back.' He gave an involuntary shiver at the thought. 'And as for this Stone Age boy, I've not seen him – but then maybe I've not been in the right place at the right time.' He thought a moment. 'All right,' he said. 'If that's the way it is, and that's what you intend, and you believe in this Kaa, well I can be in the right place too. One more day or night up there won't do me any harm.'

He towered over Johnny. 'I expect you'd squeal your head off if I tried to take the necklace off you now – I'm pretty sure it's round your neck. It's sure to be. You're just playing some child's game. But remember, Johnny, you're going to have to guard that necklace every inch you travel today and you're not going to find that very easy or pleasant. Thanks for the information.'

He picked his wallet up, then turned and made his way next door and very decisively shut himself in. He appeared to be busy moving things about the house for the rest of the morning and without waiting for his midday meal drove off at about twelve o'clock.

Over the valley Denver visibly became more and more wintry.

Tonight it should truly be Kaa's country.

Johnny thought of the way Madge had shivered with apprehension at the thought of having to go on Denver again. Would he feel the same way too? What would it be like? As terrible as Madge had made it seem?

Daniel rang some time after dinner. There had been another time-change, but only a short one and only the chill landscape to be seen. Johnny told him about Madge's offer of money and his threats.

'Is he still next door?' Daniel asked.

'No, he drove off before we ate,' Johnny said.

'Just sit tight then and we'll see you this afternoon. It isn't far off,' Daniel added encouragingly. 'And guard the necklace.'

Mum was gardening out the front. Johnny went out to join her. The necklace was in his pocket now. Wearing it round the neck as Kaa had seemed somehow wrong. But to keep it on his person was the safest thing to do as long as he was near a grown-up he could trust. He half-regretted having brought it with him now, but this morning at the Butlers' he'd not been able to bear the thought of being parted from it, and nothing they had said had persuaded him to take it off. The special connection was between him and Kaa, so now it was found he ought to keep it. And then it meant that if – unmentionable thought – the Butlers let him down, he could go on his own.

Tired of watching Mum, Johnny went and leant against the wall by the gate and gazed down the road. It was three o'clock now, getting nearer and nearer to the fateful time. An hour and a half till Mr Butler came to fetch him. He kept checking his watch. An hour and twenty-five minutes. An hour and twenty minutes. Could it be so simple though – for Mr Butler to take him over to Yonderley and hand over the necklace? How would Madge try to interfere? He must certainly mean business. There must have been at least a hundred pounds in the wallet, so how much was he expecting to sell the necklace for? And then Kaa –

would Kaa simply let them walk up and give him the necklace? And what if the time-scheme he'd worked out was wrong and the wolf got there first?

Summerfield High Street had only an odd car moving up and down it. Twice the hourly bus came and went, then later another car appeared moving very slowly towards their end of the village. It was a taxi and the driver seemed to be looking out for a house name.

The taxi came up past the primary school, past the post office and the pub, then stopped. The driver spoke to someone across the road out weeding in the front garden too. Johnny heard the driver shout thank you, then the taxi came up the road much faster. Johnny waited for it to pass, but instead it stopped right in front of him. A very sun-tanned man got out on the far side. 'This seems to be it,' he said to the driver through his open window. 'You live here?' he asked Johnny across the car-roof. The accent was not English, though Johnny was so deep in thought that he didn't immediately place it for what it was.

'Yes,' Johnny said. 'Why?'

'Well – ' the man began hesitantly. After a quick glance up and down the road he came round the back of the taxi. 'I'm pleased to meet you, then. At a guess I'd say you were Johnny. You have the family look. I'm your Uncle Charles, Charles Madge. All the way from Australia to see you.'

'You can't be,' Johnny gasped, eyes wide.

Mum came walking quickly up the garden path towards the pair of them.

'Excuse me,' she said, 'but did I heard you say Charles Madge?'

'Why yes,' the other Charles Madge said, very taken aback by this unwelcoming reception from his two relatives. 'I am Charles Madge.'

'I hope you can prove it,' Mum said grimly. 'We've someone of your name here already.'

Mum didn't wait till Dad got home. A quick glance at the 'real'

Charles Madge's passport was enough (they'd never thought to check the first's!) – she 'broke in' next door using the spare-key. Inside everything was packed up ready to take away. That was what this morning's activity had been about. Nothing of Charles Madge's – the first Charles Madge, that is, and no one knew any better name to call him by – remained in the drawers or on the shelves. Everything he'd brought into the house had been packed away. The suitcases were lined up in the front room.

'At least he was tidy, but when he comes back to pick this lot up,' Mum said, 'I'm going to give him what for. I'm almost looking forward to it. What an incredible cheek! Fancy walking into someone's house and masquerading as a relative! And it worked too.' She laughed. 'It worked very well indeed! He treated us like a hotel. You aren't married, are you, by any chance?' she said to the real Charles Madge.

'I'm going to be, very shortly,' he said. 'Why?'

'Just a confusion Johnny's Dad got the imposter into once!' Mum said. 'Do you remember, Johnny?'

Johnny nodded. He remembered. Vividly. And Melbourne.

'Surely the police would be interested,' the real Charles Madge said. He was most upset.

'I'm sure they will be,' Mum agreed. She re-locked the door. 'I don't know what game he was up to, but I hope our finding out has messed it up. Yes, I will phone the police after I've phoned Johnny's Dad. Only a criminal would try something like this.'

'But who can he be?' the real Uncle Charles was saying anxiously as they got back in the kitchen. 'He doesn't sound like anyone I know.'

'A photo! There's a photo of him!' Mum said. 'It was the last picture on the roll. I collected them from the chemist's in the village this morning when Johnny was down the farm. I haven't looked at them properly but I'm sure the one I took of him came out. Oh, where are they?'

Eventually the photos were found.

The real Uncle Charles pored over them. He thought

carefully.

'Yes, I do know him,' he said. 'Now, where did I meet him? Yes, on a plane in the Outback about six months ago. He said he was collecting aboriginal sculptures – a kind of dealer he was, in art and archaeological things. He got interested when I started talking about where my family came from, Summerfield and Yonderley and so on. I told him a story that's been in the family for years – you probably know it as well as I do. Some lad, way back, two hundred years or more, who had a strange ghostly experience. Something to do with a canal tunnel that goes under . . . you'll know the name of the hill better than I do.'

'Denver's the only hill round here that answers to that description,' Mum said.

'Denver? Probably. Well, to cut a long story short, this lad swore blind there was a ghost over the Yonderley side, and that it needed something returned to it. No one believed him of course. In fact the lad got turned off the job because of it – not that it did the canal builders any good. Something strange happened to the weather – '

'It turned wintry,' Johnny said in growing excitement. 'There were two years of winter.'

'You do know the story already,' Uncle Charles said, a little disappointed.

'I guessed it,' Johnny said. 'But does that mean that Dad and I are descendants of this boy?'

'Why yes – let's see. He'd be your great-great-great-grandfather. The lad who said he saw the ghost went out to Australia. He grew up and had a family. One of his sons came back to settle in Summerfield; the other stayed out there.'

'And did you tell this man all about us?' Johnny asked.

'I'm afraid I did,' the real Charles Madge said. 'Including your names. He told me he was going back to England in a few days and he was interested, so naturally I kept talking. I'm sorry I did, but you know how boring these long plane journeys get. And the man said he'd read some such story in an old book he owned and he had to visit the district anyway – some other business he had coming off. For whatever reasons he obviously decided to stay without paying hotel bills. I probably told him to go and look you up and mention my name if he was interested in the story.'

'Whatever he's up to, it's obviously no good,' Mum said. 'I'm phoning your father now to see what he thinks we should do.' She went through to the hall.

Johnny could see a reason now why Charles Madge – the imposter – should have come to visit them. Maybe he'd thought that if one member of their family had been able to communicate with Kaa, another in a later generation might be able to too. He would have already known about the magic necklace from the book . . . then he'd visited Yonderley when he was in the district anyway and he'd found the cave had been opened up . . .

Luck had certainly been with Charles Madge, or whatever his real name was.

The phone rang for Johnny before the police had arrived. Charles Madge hadn't shown up either, which was best for him, considering the mood Mum was in.

It was Daniel on the phone. Johnny suddenly realised what time it was. Nearly half past four.

'We're setting off to pick you up in ten minutes,' Daniel said. 'Everything all right your end? Kept the necklace safely?'

'The most unbelievable thing's happened . . .'

Johnny never finished his sentence for without warning the line went dead. Johnny dialled Daniel back, but the line to the farm remained obstinately dead.

There was only one explanation why that should be. The time-change had begun, the important one.

A thick sweater, ridiculous in this weather, tied round his neck and a torch pushed into the waist-band of his trousers, Johnny bumped his bike down the step from the back-gate into the lane, threw a leg over it and launched himself down the hill. The police had just arrived at the front of the house, but Johnny didn't wait to see what they were going to do. Round the first corner, the second and the third he tore. He was into the straight part before the bridge when he raised his head and saw that a Land Rover was parked in the turning to the Butlers'. The Butlers had come out to meet him after all. Perhaps the line had gone dead for altogether other reasons. Johnny crossed the bridge. The Land Rover started up – Johnny heard the cough of the ignition. It began turning out. That alerted him to danger for they would have no reason to meet him there. But it was too late to brake properly. He wobbled as he slowed down, but before he'd stopped completely Madge's Land Rover had run with a crunch into his front wheel.

Johnny spun off his bike and onto the narrow grass verge.

The next minute was a mad scramble – a scramble to get on his feet before Madge reached him, and a scramble to get past Madge who had stalled the Land Rover in the middle of the lane and jumped straight out.

Johnny darted up the lane towards the Butlers' drive and turned into it. Ahead he could see their gate, a hundred and fifty long yards away. Madge reached the drive too – Johnny heard the sound of his footsteps change as he came off the tarmac onto the gravel – and began pounding after him. Nearer and nearer the rasping sound of Madge's breathing came. As if in some horrible nightmarish dream Madge began to overtake. He came so near that any moment Johnny expected his hands on his shoulders. But suddenly Johnny was in sight of the front of the farm-house. That gave him a fresh burst of speed. He spied the Butlers' faces at the farmhouse window through the sweat that was running into his eyes. Madge came to a halt behind him. He ran on. He was safe!

Then the totally unexpected happened.

19

It grew darker by the cave but Kaa's eyes were cat's eyes tonight; and not a blade of grass moved in the deserted valley below or a pine cone fell to the ground among the trees on the valley rim without him knowing it. But wolves pad softly in the darkness and blend with the background. Kaa had seen them appear as though by magic from the grass in the winter weather, raiding the village flocks, and this was no time to relax, not even for a second. So he knew at once when the stranger appeared on the far side of the wooded hill. His heart quavered for a moment with the shock of it, but then he realised –

Madge had fallen behind, but Johnny tumbled over. The ground in front of him disappeared, then re-adjusted itself and found a different level. He landed painfully – not on the gravelled drive but on rock-solid ground.

Johnny twisted round where he lay, ready to fend Madge off. Surely he would take advantage of his having stumbled over. But there was no Madge there, just a way through tufted grass, beyond that a few bent pines and, still further, Summerfield Hill, utterly bare.

Bewildered, he pulled himself up into a sitting position. A quick glance in every direction told him what had happened – the all-important time-change had come already. And it was growing dark – in fact it was almost night. In the murky light

Denver as far as the eye carried was covered with pines instead of the usual beech or oak. An occasional branch sparkled for a moment with frost. Nothing moved – not even a solitary bird among the branches.

Then Johnny realised something else. The farm – he should still have seen the farm. He jumped to his feet. All he could see was a misty clearing into which the track ran through a scattering of pines. But the farm had been there yesterday in the middle of the change. He'd been there to see it. And he'd just seen the Butlers' faces at the window!

Half-stumbling, half-running, Johnny went in the direction where the farmhouse should have been. Should have been, but definitely wasn't. He reached the right-hand edge of the clearing and checked: no farm-house, no Daniel, no Butlers. Only a kind of low-lying mist that made the trees opposite indistinct. He stumbled on. The farm had to appear. It had to. It was just some trick of the light. He reached the point where he judged the gates had stood, but they weren't there; and nor were the buildings that should have been beyond it and that had survived through the time-change yesterday. Nothing was there that should have been. The time-change must have swept away the farm and the Butlers with it.

The ground was frosted stone-hard on the top, but underneath it was marshy. Veering off towards the centre of the clearing Johnny put a foot wrong and sank ankle-deep through the crust of the earth into sucking spongy mud beneath. In panic he scrambled back to the faint path and stood gasping for breath on the firmer ground.

Then came a vivid reminder of why he was there. Kaa's wolf howled, the loneliest sound on earth for Johnny. Its echo answered it so that the animal seemed to be on all sides at once. The sound ran round Denver. When it died away the wind whipped up, swaying the tops of the pines so that they made a sawing noise in the air.

Safety. Where would safety be? His brain refused to work. He stumbled and ran round the clearing, avoiding the centre which was obviously just treacherous marsh. Even so his feet plunged further and further into the soggy ground each time he took a step on the track itself.

Then he was on firmer ground, among the pines. He ran uphill as he'd never run before. It was for his life. The sound of his gasping breath was so loud in his ears that a gun going off near him would not have made the slightest impression. The rhythm of his running pounded through his head. He was aware of nothing but the running and the trees swaying above him. His sense of direction had gone; his eyes were blinded with tears of sweat. He was so unaware of where he was going that he didn't see the fallen tree in his way till the last moment. He fell over it with a crash that knocked him unconscious. The last impression he had was of the jagged wolf claws in his pocket cutting cruelly into his leg.

Kaa heard the wolf howl again. He stiffened at the cave-entrance and took his attention away from the stranger on the far side of the hill. For Kaa too the howl echoed, but he was trained to hunt and without difficulty he sorted out where it came from.

The wolf was nearer than the last time it had bayed, but it was still far away along the crest of the wooded hill. Kaa threw out his mind to the stranger again, but the stranger was in terror, only thoughts of flight and safety in his mind –

What use was such help to him?

When Johnny regained consciousness it was completely dark. He lay there trying to make sense of the darkness, of his aching head, of the thing in his pocket that was cutting the flesh at the top of his leg. Then he remembered, and he remembered too what Madge had said: 'You don't know what it's like when it changes back', and how Madge had given a kind of involuntary shiver at the thought of having to go back in time again.

Kaa – what was Kaa to him? And how could he go on alone without Daniel or Mr Butler? It was wrong to expect him to. A kind of hatred of Kaa came over him – let Madge have the necklace. What was it to him if Kaa got it back or not? If I was able to run so easily from the present into the past, Johnny thought, why can't I do it the other way round?

He scrambled to his feet and began running down the hill between the trees. In the darkness the trees seemed closer together, to lean over him, to whisper to one another. And it was difficult to avoid them – he was buffeted from one to another as he ran. It was as if each tree had arms that reached out to grasp him and throw him to the next.

In the end he stopped, panting and more in despair than ever. He leant against a trunk and listened to the wind roar through the top of the wood. The sharp necklace crushed against his leg, reproaching him. He took it out of his pocket and weighed it in his hand. He would be fair. He would not take it back for Madge to get. He would leave it here. That at least gave Kaa a chance of finding it. He raised his arm, ready to throw.

Then suddenly he couldn't do it, not leave Kaa to his fate so easily. He returned the necklace to his pocket and after a moment's hesitation grimly set his face uphill again.

On the ledge in front of the cave Kaa felt Johnny's will harden. But then he became aware that some fresh danger was approaching him from the mouth of the little valley.

Johnny reached the top of Denver. On an ordinary night he would have looked down on the lights of Summerfield and the sky beyond would have gleamed with the lights of the town where Dad worked. But tonight it didn't, and tonight there was not a solitary light below. The wind blew icily so high and Johnny crouched in the lee of a bush to try and get a bit of shelter before starting across the flat top towards the descent to Yonderley – or where Yonderley should have been.

He thought over what he had to do. He had to make his way down the steep Yonderley side of the hill and find the cave.

There was no chance of climbing down the cliffs so he would have to go all the way down along the valley-rim almost to where the present-day lane ran, then come back up the valley. Madge would be waiting for him. He couldn't believe Madge had given up his hopes of getting the necklace entirely. He could only have stopped because Johnny had run so close to the farm. Perhaps like Johnny he'd seen the Butlers' faces in the window. And then there was the wolf.

Suddenly, he saw a light flickering among the trees below him, the light of a torch. Madge had come looking for him. He jumped to his feet to run.

But it was better than that. Next he heard his own name being called low and cautiously. It could only be one person. He ran down to meet him, calling as he ran, almost tearful with joy.

'There you are,' Daniel said. 'Why didn't you wait for me?'

20

Kaa cowered within himself. He crouched motionless. Even his heart-beat slowed. He could fight the wolf, but he did not understand the figure – the person – the thing – that stood at the foot of the rocky pile that led down below the cave to the valley bottom. It filled him with terror. Madge took no notice of Kaa, however, beyond a long suspicious glance up the rocks that probably did not even find Kaa's dark crouched figure. Kaa was no concern of his. Instead Madge stood facing out down the valley. He had better things to do than worry about Stone Age savages. The whole mystery of Kaa's appearance in modern times didn't interest him. He hadn't even tried to take it in. He had to have the necklace. It meant money and he needed money of the kind he was likely to get for it. He needed it enough to do virtually anything for it . . . If only he'd taken it off that child this morning. What could his parents have done? Nothing. He was well able to cover his tracks.

Above Kaa and Madge, three-quarters of a mile away the two boys walked through the trees on the downward slope that led towards Yonderley, or where Yonderley would lie many thousands of years in the future. The keen wind which blew made them shiver even though they were wrapped up in several layers of the sweaters which Daniel had thought to bring with him.

'It's amazing down there,' Daniel was saying, a vague figure beside Johnny in the darkness. 'Just before I managed to sneak off Dad took the Land Rover down to the road. From our house it was pitch dark, then wham! we were in blinding sunlight and pitching about all over the place because the ground's changed levels over the years. To anyone outside the hill looks normal, but just cross that line and you're in for a shock.'

'I still don't know how I missed you,' Johnny said. 'I just can't get over it. I didn't expect to see you again, ever.'

'Dad's got a theory about what happened,' Daniel explained. 'He thinks our farm's built in a natural clearing of the wood. There never were trees there, probably because it was so marshy. Even now we have trouble with springs.'

'But why didn't I see you?' Johnny said. 'The rest doesn't matter.'

'Dad reckons,' Daniel said matter-of-factly as if they were walking across the school playing-fields, 'the whole wood has slipped back in time. It looks normal from outside, but as soon as you pass inside the limits of the old wood you pass backwards through a barrier of thousands of years. Our house is surrounded by the old wood and the old time so we can see it even if we're still in the present – but looking from the old time into ours isn't possible, because our time didn't exist then. Kaa didn't see us, nor did you. And that's why we could see you as you went running up the side of the clearing, but you couldn't see us. You can't imagine how odd it was to see you charging past the house not even knowing we were there. But the same thing happened to us in the Land Rover – we had to drive straight into that marshy clearing to find our house.'

'You thought it was odd!' Johnny said. 'Didn't you do anything? I thought Kaa's wolf was creeping up on me.'

'Do anything? Of course we did,' Daniel said. 'We were out of the door and shouting our heads off as soon as we realised who you were, but it was too late. You couldn't hear us by then. And it was all over in a minute or two, even if it seemed like a life-time to you. I was going to chase after you, but Dad wouldn't let me go.'

'But I was so near!'

'I know, but Dad grabbed hold of me. I properly fought him to let me go.' Daniel stopped a moment to think of that. 'Mind you, he meant for the best. He said no one else was going to risk their lives. He said you'd realise your mistake in a minute and come back, or try to reach the road. He didn't know you thought you were being chased.'

'Your Dad was right really,' Johnny said thoughtfully. 'If I'd had any sense I wouldn't have panicked, but then as I told you Madge chased me up the track to the farm. That wasn't the best of starts for finding my way.'

'The ground's starting to go down,' Daniel observed, speaking more quietly than he had before. 'We'd better start thinking of what's going to happen, not of what's gone on. And remember how worried Kaa's father was that Kaa would blunder over the cliff-face.'

Johnny slowed down, remembering that too.

They felt their way from tree to tree in silence. Ahead was pitch-black and more than once they lost contact with one another. The dirt was loose under their feet and they kept slipping forward down the slope, which was terrifying knowing what might lie ahead. The only sound was that of their feet being cautiously raised and lowered, and of the wind in the high tree-tops.

Daniel stopped and whispered. 'We ought to use our torches,' he said.

'No, not unless it's absolutely necessary,' Johnny whispered back. 'If we do, Madge will spot us coming.'

'If one of us lands with a thud at the bottom of the cliff he'll know only too well. And we're moving too slowly. The wolf's supposed to arrive after dark and it's been dark for ages.'

'We'll just have to be even more careful than we have been already,' Johnny said.

'I'll go first then,' Daniel said, 'if you mean to be so careless with your own life.'

They were moving at a snail's pace. Five minutes passed, ten. They seemed to be getting nowhere. The ground went down unendingly. Impatient Johnny forgot the danger and suddenly began to forge ahead again. 'Careful!' Daniel cautioned more loudly than he should have. A moment later Johnny carefully put his front foot down – on nothing. For a second he stood on one leg with his body suspended in mid-air. He clearly heard some stones and dirt hit the ground at the foot of the cliff below him. Then Daniel pulled him back.

'I told you!' Daniel whispered harshly. He held Johnny on the ground. 'Now, just don't move until you've recovered.'

A minute later Johnny dared to look. As his eyes gradually accustomed themselves to the quality of the darkness he began to see broad outlines of what lay below and ahead of them. The cliffs, whiter than they seemed to have been in their own time, loomed out over on the right – the cave was somewhere there, though the piles of rocks that lay in front of the cliffs were just a confused jumble. Nor could Johnny see the details of what was below. Madge might be anywhere down there. On the other hand he might not have come at all.

Then Kaa was in Johnny's mind.

Kaa crouched on the little ledge of rock in front of his cave. He knew that his helper was on the hill and with him a companion. That was to be expected. He knew too that the wolf after its wide circle over the nearby hills in search of food was coming back to him and was quite close now. But there was the other fear. In the valley bottom was another person, so close that Kaa had the smell of him in his nostrils and Kaa did not know who that person was. But he did know he was there to do him no good.

And then there was a sharp clink of sound Kaa did not understand at all.

Suddenly Johnny was back in his own head.

'What's up?' Daniel said. 'Snap out of it, Johnny!' He was shaking his friend.

'Kaa,' Johnny said weakly. 'Down there. He's never come on this strong before.'

'What?'

'Something's happening. I don't know what. Look for me.'

'There is something. It's a lamp – no, a large torch,' Daniel said. 'It's moving about as if someone is searching for something on the ground. He's found it – no, he hasn't.'

Johnny struggled upright to look too.

'Madge!' he said. 'That's what Kaa's heard. He is there and he must have dropped something.'

The torch light moved methodically to and fro over a small area of ground, then they heard an unmistakable grunt of satisfaction. The torch was placed on the ground and a hand and an arm up to the elbow appeared in the light before it was switched off. Then there was another flare of light that lit up Madge's face – at least it must have been his face for what they saw was more like a Hallowe'en mask. A cigarette glowed in the darkness.

'He dropped his lighter,' Johnny said. 'Fancy risking attracting the wolf just for the sake of that.'

'The wolf almost certainly knows all about him by smell anyway,' Daniel said. 'And all about us too, come to think of it.'

'We've got to get down there,' Johnny whispered. 'There's no time to waste. Come on – let's go up the bank then follow the valley rim round. It shouldn't be too difficult, and it'll be safer.' He clambered to his feet and swayed to gain his balance above the fall.

'No!' Daniel pulled him back excitedly. 'Wait a moment. I think our problem's partly solved. Look to the right.'

There was a glow in the sky lighting the side of one of the clouds.

'The time-change is ending!' Johnny said. He was filled with despair. All they'd done had been to no avail.

'No, it's not that! The moon's risen and there's a gap in the clouds.' Daniel pointed. 'Look!'

Daniel was right. It was a full round moon, large and near as it sailed into view. The clouds seemed to part before it. A velvet darkness lined the sky while below down the steep hill slope the moonlight picked out detail after detail as if an arc-light had been set up over the scene. Madge came into full view before he removed himself into the shadow. He was standing at the foot of the slope they knew well for half-way up it was the cave, its actual mouth hidden by a line of rock which Johnny didn't remember – probably it had been dynamited away by the canal builders.

'We can see well enough now,' Daniel said. 'Let's go. We'll be at the mouth of the valley in five minutes' time.'

But Johnny lingered. He fancied he could actually see Kaa, a dot away across the valley.

'*Come on*!' Daniel urged. 'Remember that wolf!'

Sooner than Daniel had predicted they reached the limits of the cottage garden in present-day times, but there were no trees between them and the cliffs which surrounded them. Kaa was fully in sight now, still as a statue gazing out over the valley, though occasionally he turned his head to look up to the top of the cliff. Madge was on sentry-duty below, his eyes darting here there and everywhere.

It was the first time Johnny had ever been able to think: 'If I was over there by Kaa, I could touch him, I could talk to him,' and that was a strange and marvellous thought.

'If Madge is between us and Kaa,' Daniel whispered, 'how are we going to get past?'

'He's stronger than us on our own, but not both of us together,' Johnny said. 'That must give us a chance.'

The moon shone straight down into the little valley, painting everything either an impenetrable black or a glowing white. The light shone off Madge's glasses as he waited at the foot of the rock-pile, but his face was a cavernous darkness.

'Wolves can move really fast if they want to,' Daniel said anxiously. 'It might be here any moment.'

Over at the bottom of the rocks Madge shifted uneasily from foot to foot. He was wrapped up very very warm and his figure was formidably bulky from a distance. He glanced up at the ledge, then scanned the way up the valley again. He knew as well as Johnny and Daniel did that this was the only way the boys could come short of climbing down the cliff by rope. There was a chance they wouldn't come of course, but Madge thought they would – Johnny was very obstinate. The sooner they came the better – then this ridiculous business would be over and he could get away from Yonderley and Summerfield and back to London.

Flat on his stomach Johnny squirmed along the ground nearer and nearer to the foot of the cliff. Madge for all his watching didn't notice him or Daniel close behind. No more than thirty yards from Madge Johnny stopped behind a rock and cautiously raised his head. He looked towards Kaa.

Kaa was slight and seemed about Johnny's height, much shorter than Daniel. Furs swathed his body, but his head was bare and even in the moonlight everything about him was dark; his skin, his hair, his eyes. His nose was squat and wide, his lips thick. His hair fell down to his shoulders.

'I'm here,' Johnny said with his mind.

'I know,' Kaa answered almost instantly. 'Have you got the necklace?'

'Yes,' Johnny replied.

Kaa's eyes seemed to glitter as he looked down over the rocks to the valley floor and located Johnny and Daniel.

'My father said you would come,' Kaa whispered.

Then besides Madge there was something else dangerous on the hillside.

Madge strained to hear the sounds of the night. He liked being where he was less and less as time went on – he had had to virtually force himself across the time-barrier on the towpath.

After several nights spent on the prehistoric hillside only the thought of the money had kept him going. He hated this near-silent landscape he didn't understand. He would have liked to have had a gun to shatter the silvery moon that made the valley and hillside so mysterious and ghostly.

Brushwood crackled among the trees on the top of the cliff above the cave. Madge's head swivelled. The children! Then he gave a gasp of fear.

On the ledge Kaa stood up straight, spear in hand, and calmly turned to gaze up above his head. It had come at last then.

Down on the valley floor Daniel and Johnny held their breath.

Out from among the trees and into the moonlight on the very edge of the cliff a wolf stepped. It was larger than any Johnny had ever seen before, though only Kaa could appreciate the majesty of its size. Its eyes gleamed as its breath clouded the air.

The wolf stood gazing down, taking in all it saw. It felt no need to stay hidden for it was master of the situation. After its gaze around it lowered its head, sniffing at the ground. It was searching for the way down to Kaa. It knew there was a way for its sense of smell told it that the boy had climbed down the cliff wall that day. In a moment it had sniffed out the spot. It tested it with one of its front paws. It was hungry, ravenously hungry, for it had not eaten properly for several days. It had no intention of being baulked of its prey.

Johnny jumped to his feet. He fumbled in his pocket and pulled out the necklace. He knew that Kaa had to have it before he faced the wolf if he was to prove himself worthy of his priesthood.

At the foot of the cliff Madge, by now in terror for he'd known nothing about the wolf before, sensed more movement down the valley and turned and saw Johnny with the necklace in his hand. Seeing Johnny he almost fell over in his eagerness to cut him off. At last here was his chance to get hold of what he'd dreamt of for so long. He could already see all the money it represented. He even managed to forget the wolf for those brief seconds of triumph. He knew that Johnny had no choice but to come forward if he was ever to give it to Kaa, and he knew that that was what Johnny was set on. The fact that Daniel was running wildly after Johnny didn't worry Madge.

Kaa knew without being told that the figure running and stumbling towards the cliffs in the moonlight was the one who had come to help him and that the figure below whose presence had so terrified him was his enemy. Above Kaa the wolf had planted two sure feet on a narrow ledge and was preparing to slither the rest of the way down.

Kaa hurriedly slung the spear onto the shelf above the cave and scrambled after it. He was now no more than three spears' length from the wolf, so close that he felt its warm breath on the frosty air. The wolf looked down on him, for a second or two unable to come down or go back. For that moment Kaa could have chosen to kill the wolf, but he did not choose. He left the wolf for a fair fight. His first wolf, his priest's wolf, must be killed face to face, equal chance to animal and boy. And below him something even more important than his own individual life was waiting for him and maybe at the last moment was going to be snatched away. He would rather be dead than lose that.

Johnny faced Madge.

'You tried hard,' Madge panted, glancing back over his shoulder towards the wolf and Kaa. 'Now I've got you. Give it here.'

Johnny tried to dodge past him, but an outstretched hand put paid to that. He fell back out of Madge's reach.

'Here,' Daniel said close by Johnny's elbow. 'Let me have it. He can't stop both of us.'

'Your mothers and fathers will never see either of you again at this rate,' Madge threatened. Part of his attention was still directed over his shoulder. 'Give it me now.'

'It's Kaa's,' Johnny shouted. 'You'll never have it.'

'Give it to me,' Daniel pleaded. 'He can't stop both of us.'

'I can't,' Johnny said. 'I've got to give it to Kaa.'

Madge advanced on Johnny and Johnny retreated. Daniel darted between the pair of them, but Madge brushed him aside. Johnny turned, but Madge caught him by his free arm. He pulled Johnny back towards him and wrenched him round. 'Mine,' Madge said, 'and no one else's.' He pulled Johnny's other hand that held the necklace towards him . . .

Kaa raced down the spur of rock towards the bottom of the rock-pile. One foot wrong and he would have gone flying onto the rocks below and broken his back.

Ahead he saw Madge twist and wrench Johnny's arm so that the necklace fell out of his grasp onto the ground. He saw Madge send Johnny sprawling on the ground, his face twisted with pain, and felt in his mind Johnny's regret and despair. He saw Madge throw Daniel aside as Daniel again attempted to stop him and then pick the necklace up.

Madge shook himself, took one last look over his shoulder, then ran for the trees and the mouth of the valley. He had seen how close Kaa was to the bottom of the rocks.

Kaa reached the valley floor. In one swift movement he raised the spear and threw it after the receding figure of Madge. He flung it low and, as it passed over his head, Johnny thought it would strike Madge in the body and kill him, but at the last moment it dipped and passed between Madge's legs. Entangled on the spear Madge fell to the ground.

For a moment no one moved. Even the wolf was still.

Johnny looked up and met Kaa's eyes. He could not read them as he had read his mind. But there was one more service Johnny knew he could do for Kaa. He scrambled painfully to his feet and hobbled over to the terrified Madge. From under his fingers he removed the sharp-clawed necklace. Madge didn't resist.

Slowly Johnny took the necklace to Kaa. As Kaa took it their fingers touched briefly. They weren't a ghost's fingers, but real solid fingers. Kaa hung the necklace round his neck, the place it should be, then looked at Johnny – looked *up* at Johnny. The

Stone Age boy was even shorter than Johnny was. Johnny almost laughed. In his imagination he'd always thought of Kaa as tall because he was so brave. Johnny wet his lips. His throat was dry. He wanted to say something, to do something, but at the last moment there was nothing more to do and nothing more to say. He looked away.

'The wolf!' Daniel whispered from where he lay.

The wolf had at last slithered down to the shelf on the cliff. Then faster than anything Johnny had ever seen before it was on its way down the spur of rock towards them, leaping, almost flying in its eagerness.

Kaa pushed Johnny out of his way and darted towards Madge. Madge cowered, but it wasn't him Kaa was after. Kaa scooped up the spear from where it had fallen and ran back past Johnny towards the wolf which was already at the foot of the rocks.

Neither Kaa nor the wolf slackened pace as they ran together.

Kaa and the wolf met. There was the sound of the spear-shaft breaking and splintering. Part of it flew into the air. The air was full of the wolf's snarls and Kaa's cries of defiance. Johnny and Daniel saw the wolf on top of the boy's body, its head down and its jaws working. Briefly Kaa was uppermost, but the animal thrashed itself on top of the boy and worked away with its jaws again.

Yet when everything seemed lost the wolf turned over on its side, its eyes piteously rolling. Kaa had wounded it after all when they'd first come together. But Kaa . . . had he . . . Johnny rushed towards him.

Without noticing Johnny, Kaa struggled slowly to his feet and knelt wearily over the wolf's body. He tugged at the broken spear-shaft which all the time had been impaled in the animal's chest. In a rush of blood the spear-head came out.

Kaa had killed his first wolf! He had proved his priesthood!

He pulled a short knife out of his belt and cut off the right forepaw of the wolf. He stowed it in a fold of his furs that seemed to do as a pocket and then tossed the bloodied, broken-off spear-head away high into the moonlight. It fell with a clatter on the rocks below the cave.

For a moment he knelt in prayer for his dead father, then seconds later he was gone, away among the trees down towards the mouth of the valley, moving south, going home, the necklace proudly round his neck.

Johnny called after him: 'Kaa!'

Faintly, in his mind, there seemed to come the echo of a goodbye.

Postscript

'Well I'll be blowed!' Dad said one Sunday after dinner that autumn. 'See if you recognise who this is.'

He read from the newspaper.

CHARLES MAXELL: SUPER CONMAN

Ex-actor, ex-journalist, ex-antique dealer, con-man Charles Maxell was jailed for five years at Exeter County Court this week. He was convicted of stealing three valuable Chinese vases from a widow to whom he posed as an employee from the British Museum. Maxell obtained the vases by pretending the Museum required them for valuation. Maxell asked for nineteen other cases to be taken into consideration.

Maxell was apprehended by the police for driving a Land Rover at excessive speed. The Land Rover, it transpired, was wanted by the police. It had been fraudulently obtained by Maxell in Gloucester. The defendant had used stolen credit cards to acquire it.

Charles Maxell, alias Charles Madge, alias Peter Sitwell, alias Derek Bate, has led a chequered life. A soldier in the British Army, dismissed for misappropriating mess funds, he worked as an actor for several years after leaving the Army, then in journalism in Australia. Subsequently he set himself up as an antique dealer in the West End of London, dealing in out-of-the-way objects that police say were more often than not obtained illegally. He is currently wanted by Australian police in connection with thefts from a valuable collection of Aboriginal art.

Mrs d'Arcy, the lady defrauded of her vases, said that Maxell had produced documents claiming he was a British Museum employee. She also said he spoke with a foreign accent and said he was Chief Keeper of Chinese Antiquities.

'Is that all?' Mum said.

'How much did you want?' Dad said. 'Now at least we know who the fellow was, even if we don't really know why he boarded himself on us. And we know where to send his luggage.'

Dad looked over at Johnny. He wrinkled up his brow.

'We've not asked much since that evening Mr Butler and his Ministry of Agriculture friend brought you back saying you could probably do with a good night's rest because you'd had some odd experience, but maybe you'd like to tell us now,' Dad said. He looked over to Mum for confirmation.

'It's a long story, but I want to tell you,' Johnny said. 'I'm not sure you're going to believe all of it.'

His mind flew back to that night at the start of the holidays over at Yonderley – to how heart-broken he'd felt as Kaa disappeared for ever among the trees – to how Mr Butler and his friend had come running up the valley, shot-guns in hand to rescue him and Daniel – to how they had stood in wonder looking down at the huge wolf – to how in the confusion Madge had slipped away, not to be heard of again till now –

'It started the weekend before we broke up at school,' Johnny began, 'the day Daniel was testing his new bike . . .'